This book belongs to

Adams media

Adams Media
An Imprint of Simon & Schuster, Inc.
100 Technology Center Drive
Stoughton, Massachusetts 02072

First Adams Media hardcover edition June 2021

ADAMS MEDIA and colophon are trademarks of Simon & Schuster.

For information about special discounts for bulk purchases, please contact Simon & Schuster Special Sales at 1-866-506-1949 or business@simonandschuster.com.

The Simon & Schuster Speakers Bureau can bring authors to your live event. For more information or to book an event contact the Simon & Schuster Speakers Bureau at 1-866-248-3049 or visit our website at www.simonspeakers.com.

Interior design and illustrations by Priscilla Yuen

Manufactured in the United States of America

1 2021

ISBN 978-1-5072-1648-4

the
good
morning
journal

5-Minute Guided Reflections to Start Your Day with Inspiration, Purpose, and a Plan

Introduction by Molly Burford
Author of *The No Worries Workbook*

ADAMS MEDIA
New York London Toronto Sydney New Delhi

introduction

Ah, mornings. A new beginning. A fresh start. With every sunrise comes an invigorating opportunity—each day is a new chance to start again and give it your personal best.

But every great opportunity still needs a plan in order to see itself through. A wonderful way for you to make this happen is to create a morning routine that's structured with success, productivity, and, most of all, happiness. The usual list items like waking up on time, immediately brushing your teeth, and taking a brisk walk are all awesome activities to engage in first thing. But the best one? A reflective journaling practice. This is exactly what *The Good Morning Journal* is for!

In only 5 minutes, this little guide will help you start your day off in a way that's reflective, intentional, and organized. By taking the small amount of time required to fill in this journal's pages, you will find yourself far more productive and definitely more *inspired*! It's only 5 minutes—that's 300 seconds—all about *you*. You're worth that time, and then some.

In this journal, you will:

- *Track how you feel upon waking (rested, overwhelmed, cheerful, angry, and so on)*
- *Plan for how you want to feel upon going to bed*
- *Write out how you want to spend every precious hour*

- *Fill in journal prompts*
- *Find inspirational quotes*
- *Rate your day overall*
- *And more!*

The Good Morning Journal helps keep your days on track. Use the journal whenever and wherever works for you—it's your morning after all! Filling in this journal will focus and motivate you so you can move through your morning and into your day with a positive mindset. Even if you aren't someone who likes to rise with the sun, you can definitely wake up a few minutes earlier to ensure you get your pages in. In fact, you might even find that you look forward to your alarm with this new practice!

Your time is most useful when you create a plan for how it will be spent. But it's not all about productivity and work; it's about your *life* too! As you schedule in the essential obligations and to-dos, don't forget to include the fun things too. Time to focus on a hobby or interest. A coffee break. A phone call or meetup with a loved one. Even just time to daydream. Write it all down. Make time for whatever you want to prioritize and focus on—no matter how big or how small.

At the end of the day, you have a chance to reflect on your day and all you accomplished. If you didn't meet all your goals, that's okay. Focus on progress instead of perfection. If you fell short, reflect on why and decide how you can make more progress the next day. Be gentle with yourself and make sure your expectations and plans are realistic. Also be sure to celebrate your successes and give yourself credit for what you did accomplish.

No matter how you choose to spend your morning, make it the best it can be!

Happy planning!

Date / /

THIS MORNING, I FEEL						AT THE END OF TODAY, I WANT TO FEEL					
	slightly			very			slightly			very	
Calm						Productive					
Rested						Happy					
Cheerful						Fulfilled					
Confident						Inspired					
Focused						Free					
Tired						Relaxed					
Emotional						Strong					
Stressed						In control					
Overwhelmed						Content					
Angry						Relieved					

This morning, I feel _____ because _____

_____

To feel _____ at the end of the day, I will choose to prioritize

1 _____

2 _____

3 _____

To honor my priorities, I will

1 _____

2 _____

3 _____

Three things I want to accomplish today

1 _____

2 _____

3 _____

To complete these goals, I will

1 _____

2 _____

3 _____

THIS IS HOW I PLAN TO USE MY TIME TODAY

I give today ☆ ☆ ☆ ☆ ☆

5 AM	
6 AM	
7 AM	
8 AM	
9 AM	
10 AM	
11 AM	
12 PM	
1 PM	
2 PM	
3 PM	
4 PM	
5 PM	
6 PM	
7 PM	
8 PM	
9 PM	
10 PM	
11 PM	
12 AM	

Tomorrow morning will be
even better because _____

_____

_____

_____

_____

_____

*Write it on your
heart that every
day is the best
day in the year.*

RALPH WALDO EMERSON,
*American philosopher
and poet*

Date / /

THIS MORNING, I FEEL	slightly			very		AT THE END OF TODAY, I WANT TO FEEL	slightly			very	
Calm						Productive					
Rested						Happy					
Cheerful						Fulfilled					
Confident						Inspired					
Focused						Free					
Tired						Relaxed					
Emotional						Strong					
Stressed						In control					
Overwhelmed						Content					
Angry						Relieved					

This morning, I feel _____ because _____

_____

To feel _____ at the end of the day, I will choose to prioritize

1 _____

2 _____

3 _____

To honor my priorities, I will

1 _____

2 _____

3 _____

Three things I want to accomplish today

1 _____

2 _____

3 _____

To complete these goals, I will

1 _____

2 _____

3 _____

THIS IS HOW I PLAN TO USE MY TIME TODAY

5 AM	
6 AM	
7 AM	
8 AM	
9 AM	
10 AM	
11 AM	
12 PM	
1 PM	
2 PM	
3 PM	
4 PM	
5 PM	
6 PM	
7 PM	
8 PM	
9 PM	
10 PM	
11 PM	
12 AM	

I give today ☆ ☆ ☆ ☆ ☆

Tomorrow morning will be
even better because _____

_____

_____

_____

_____

_____

*All those things that
you're worried about aren't
important. You're going to
be okay. Better than okay.
You're going to be great.
Spend less time tearing
yourself apart, worrying
if you're good enough.
You are good enough.*

REESE WITHERSPOON,
American actor

Date / /

THIS MORNING, I FEEL						AT THE END OF TODAY, I WANT TO FEEL					
	slightly			very			slightly			very	
Calm						Productive					
Rested						Happy					
Cheerful						Fulfilled					
Confident						Inspired					
Focused						Free					
Tired						Relaxed					
Emotional						Strong					
Stressed						In control					
Overwhelmed						Content					
Angry						Relieved					

This morning, I feel _____ because _____

_____

To feel _____ at the end of
the day, I will choose to prioritize

1 _____

2 _____

3 _____

To honor my priorities, I will

1 _____

2 _____

3 _____

Three things I want to accomplish
today

1 _____

2 _____

3 _____

To complete these goals, I will

1 _____

2 _____

3 _____

THIS IS HOW I PLAN TO USE MY TIME TODAY

5 AM	
6 AM	
7 AM	
8 AM	
9 AM	
10 AM	
11 AM	
12 PM	
1 PM	
2 PM	
3 PM	
4 PM	
5 PM	
6 PM	
7 PM	
8 PM	
9 PM	
10 PM	
11 PM	
12 AM	

I give today ☆ ☆ ☆ ☆ ☆

Tomorrow morning will be even better because _____

_____

_____

_____

_____

_____

_____

"Thank you" is the best prayer that anyone could say.

ALICE WALKER,
*American author
and activist*

Date / /

THIS MORNING, I FEEL	slightly				very		AT THE END OF TODAY, I WANT TO FEEL	slightly				very	
Calm							Productive						
Rested							Happy						
Cheerful							Fulfilled						
Confident							Inspired						
Focused							Free						
Tired							Relaxed						
Emotional							Strong						
Stressed							In control						
Overwhelmed							Content						
Angry							Relieved						

This morning, I feel _____ because _____

_____

To feel _____ at the end of the day, I will choose to prioritize

1 _____

2 _____

3 _____

To honor my priorities, I will

1 _____

2 _____

3 _____

Three things I want to accomplish today

1 _____

2 _____

3 _____

To complete these goals, I will

1 _____

2 _____

3 _____

THIS IS HOW I PLAN TO USE MY TIME TODAY

5 AM	
6 AM	
7 AM	
8 AM	
9 AM	
10 AM	
11 AM	
12 PM	
1 PM	
2 PM	
3 PM	
4 PM	
5 PM	
6 PM	
7 PM	
8 PM	
9 PM	
10 PM	
11 PM	
12 AM	

I give today ☆ ☆ ☆ ☆ ☆

Tomorrow morning will be even better because _____

_____

_____

_____

_____

_____

Do not let the behavior of others destroy your inner peace.

TENZIN GYATSO,
His Holiness the Fourteenth
Dalai Lama

Date / /

THIS MORNING, I FEEL	slightly					very		AT THE END OF TODAY, I WANT TO FEEL	slightly					very
Calm								Productive						
Rested								Happy						
Cheerful								Fulfilled						
Confident								Inspired						
Focused								Free						
Tired								Relaxed						
Emotional								Strong						
Stressed								In control						
Overwhelmed								Content						
Angry								Relieved						

This morning, I feel _____ because _____

_____

To feel _____ at the end of the day, I will choose to prioritize

1 _____

2 _____

3 _____

Three things I want to accomplish today

1 _____

2 _____

3 _____

To honor my priorities, I will

1 _____

2 _____

3 _____

To complete these goals, I will

1 _____

2 _____

3 _____

THIS IS HOW I PLAN TO USE MY TIME TODAY

5 AM	
6 AM	
7 AM	
8 AM	
9 AM	
10 AM	
11 AM	
12 PM	
1 PM	
2 PM	
3 PM	
4 PM	
5 PM	
6 PM	
7 PM	
8 PM	
9 PM	
10 PM	
11 PM	
12 AM	

I give today ☆ ☆ ☆ ☆ ☆

Tomorrow morning will be even better because _____

_____

_____

_____

_____

_____

Be in love with your life, every detail of it.

JACK KEROUAC,
American author

Date / /

THIS MORNING, I FEEL	slightly			very	AT THE END OF TODAY, I WANT TO FEEL	slightly			very
Calm					Productive				
Rested					Happy				
Cheerful					Fulfilled				
Confident					Inspired				
Focused					Free				
Tired					Relaxed				
Emotional					Strong				
Stressed					In control				
Overwhelmed					Content				
Angry					Relieved				

This morning, I feel _____ because _____

_____

To feel _____ at the end of the day, I will choose to prioritize

1 _____
2 _____
3 _____

Three things I want to accomplish today

1 _____
2 _____
3 _____

To honor my priorities, I will

1 _____
2 _____
3 _____

To complete these goals, I will

1 _____
2 _____
3 _____

THIS IS HOW I PLAN TO USE MY TIME TODAY

5 AM	
6 AM	
7 AM	
8 AM	
9 AM	
10 AM	
11 AM	
12 PM	
1 PM	
2 PM	
3 PM	
4 PM	
5 PM	
6 PM	
7 PM	
8 PM	
9 PM	
10 PM	
11 PM	
12 AM	

I give today ☆ ☆ ☆ ☆ ☆

Tomorrow morning will be
even better because _____

_____

_____

_____

_____

*When I
started counting
my blessings,
my whole life
turned around.*

WILLIE NELSON,
*American singer
and songwriter*

Date / /

THIS MORNING, I FEEL	slightly			very		AT THE END OF TODAY, I WANT TO FEEL	slightly			very	
Calm						Productive					
Rested						Happy					
Cheerful						Fulfilled					
Confident						Inspired					
Focused						Free					
Tired						Relaxed					
Emotional						Strong					
Stressed						In control					
Overwhelmed						Content					
Angry						Relieved					

This morning, I feel _____ because _____

_____

To feel _____ at the end of
the day, I will choose to prioritize

1 _____

2 _____

3 _____

Three things I want to accomplish
today

1 _____

2 _____

3 _____

To honor my priorities, I will

1 _____

2 _____

3 _____

To complete these goals, I will

1 _____

2 _____

3 _____

THIS IS HOW I PLAN TO USE MY TIME TODAY

5 AM	
6 AM	
7 AM	
8 AM	
9 AM	
10 AM	
11 AM	
12 PM	
1 PM	
2 PM	
3 PM	
4 PM	
5 PM	
6 PM	
7 PM	
8 PM	
9 PM	
10 PM	
11 PM	
12 AM	

I give today ☆ ☆ ☆ ☆ ☆

Tomorrow morning will be even better because _____

_____

_____

_____

_____

_____

The most important thing is to enjoy your life—to be happy— it's all that matters.

AUDREY HEPBURN,
*English actor and
humanitarian*

Date / /

THIS MORNING, I FEEL			slightly			very	AT THE END OF TODAY, I WANT TO FEEL			slightly			very
Calm							Productive						
Rested							Happy						
Cheerful							Fulfilled						
Confident							Inspired						
Focused							Free						
Tired							Relaxed						
Emotional							Strong						
Stressed							In control						
Overwhelmed							Content						
Angry							Relieved						

This morning, I feel _____ because _____

_____

To feel _____ at the end of the day, I will choose to prioritize

1 _____

2 _____

3 _____

To honor my priorities, I will

1 _____

2 _____

3 _____

Three things I want to accomplish today

1 _____

2 _____

3 _____

To complete these goals, I will

1 _____

2 _____

3 _____

THIS IS HOW I PLAN TO USE MY TIME TODAY

5 AM	
6 AM	
7 AM	
8 AM	
9 AM	
10 AM	
11 AM	
12 PM	
1 PM	
2 PM	
3 PM	
4 PM	
5 PM	
6 PM	
7 PM	
8 PM	
9 PM	
10 PM	
11 PM	
12 AM	

I give today ☆ ☆ ☆ ☆ ☆

Tomorrow morning will be
even better because _____

_____

_____

_____

_____

_____

_____

*Have patience
with all things,
but first of all
with yourself.*

*FRANCIS DE SALES,
sixteenth-century Roman
Catholic saint*

Date / /

THIS MORNING, I FEEL						AT THE END OF TODAY, I WANT TO FEEL					
	slightly			very			slightly			very	
Calm						Productive					
Rested						Happy					
Cheerful						Fulfilled					
Confident						Inspired					
Focused						Free					
Tired						Relaxed					
Emotional						Strong					
Stressed						In control					
Overwhelmed						Content					
Angry						Relieved					

This morning, I feel _____ because _____

_____

To feel _____ at the end of the day, I will choose to prioritize

1 _____

2 _____

3 _____

Three things I want to accomplish today

1 _____

2 _____

3 _____

To honor my priorities, I will

1 _____

2 _____

3 _____

To complete these goals, I will

1 _____

2 _____

3 _____

THIS IS HOW I PLAN TO USE MY TIME TODAY

5 AM	
6 AM	
7 AM	
8 AM	
9 AM	
10 AM	
11 AM	
12 PM	
1 PM	
2 PM	
3 PM	
4 PM	
5 PM	
6 PM	
7 PM	
8 PM	
9 PM	
10 PM	
11 PM	
12 AM	

I give today ☆ ☆ ☆ ☆ ☆

Tomorrow morning will be even better because _____

_____

_____

_____

_____

_____

The more you praise and celebrate your life, the more there is in life to celebrate.

OPRAH WINFREY,
American entrepreneur,
philanthropist, and
TV host

Date   /   /

THIS MORNING, I FEEL					AT THE END OF TODAY, I WANT TO FEEL				
	slightly		very			slightly		very	
Calm					Productive				
Rested					Happy				
Cheerful					Fulfilled				
Confident					Inspired				
Focused					Free				
Tired					Relaxed				
Emotional					Strong				
Stressed					In control				
Overwhelmed					Content				
Angry					Relieved				

This morning, I feel _____ because _____

_____

To feel _____ at the end of the day, I will choose to prioritize

1 _____

2 _____

3 _____

Three things I want to accomplish today

1 _____

2 _____

3 _____

To honor my priorities, I will

1 _____

2 _____

3 _____

To complete these goals, I will

1 _____

2 _____

3 _____

THIS IS HOW I PLAN TO USE MY TIME TODAY

5 AM	
6 AM	
7 AM	
8 AM	
9 AM	
10 AM	
11 AM	
12 PM	
1 PM	
2 PM	
3 PM	
4 PM	
5 PM	
6 PM	
7 PM	
8 PM	
9 PM	
10 PM	
11 PM	
12 AM	

I give today ☆ ☆ ☆ ☆ ☆

Tomorrow morning will be even better because _____

_____

_____

_____

_____

_____

Now and then it's good to pause in our pursuit of happiness and just be happy.

GUILLAUME APOLLINAIRE,
French poet

Date / /

THIS MORNING, I FEEL	slightly			very		AT THE END OF TODAY, I WANT TO FEEL	slightly			very
Calm						Productive				
Rested						Happy				
Cheerful						Fulfilled				
Confident						Inspired				
Focused						Free				
Tired						Relaxed				
Emotional						Strong				
Stressed						In control				
Overwhelmed						Content				
Angry						Relieved				

This morning, I feel _____ because _____

_____

To feel _____ at the end of the day, I will choose to prioritize

1 _____

2 _____

3 _____

To honor my priorities, I will

1 _____

2 _____

3 _____

Three things I want to accomplish today

1 _____

2 _____

3 _____

To complete these goals, I will

1 _____

2 _____

3 _____

THIS IS HOW I PLAN TO USE MY TIME TODAY

5 AM	
6 AM	
7 AM	
8 AM	
9 AM	
10 AM	
11 AM	
12 PM	
1 PM	
2 PM	
3 PM	
4 PM	
5 PM	
6 PM	
7 PM	
8 PM	
9 PM	
10 PM	
11 PM	
12 AM	

I give today ☆ ☆ ☆ ☆ ☆

Tomorrow morning will be
even better because _____

_____

_____

_____

_____

_____

Folks are usually about as happy as they make their minds up to be.

ABRAHAM LINCOLN,
sixteenth president of
the United States

Date / /

THIS MORNING, I FEEL						AT THE END OF TODAY, I WANT TO FEEL					
	slightly			very			slightly			very	
Calm						Productive					
Rested						Happy					
Cheerful						Fulfilled					
Confident						Inspired					
Focused						Free					
Tired						Relaxed					
Emotional						Strong					
Stressed						In control					
Overwhelmed						Content					
Angry						Relieved					

This morning, I feel _____ because _____

_____

To feel _____ at the end of
the day, I will choose to prioritize

1 _____

2 _____

3 _____

Three things I want to accomplish
today

1 _____

2 _____

3 _____

To honor my priorities, I will

1 _____

2 _____

3 _____

To complete these goals, I will

1 _____

2 _____

3 _____

THIS IS HOW I PLAN TO USE MY TIME TODAY

5 AM	
6 AM	
7 AM	
8 AM	
9 AM	
10 AM	
11 AM	
12 PM	
1 PM	
2 PM	
3 PM	
4 PM	
5 PM	
6 PM	
7 PM	
8 PM	
9 PM	
10 PM	
11 PM	
12 AM	

I give today ☆ ☆ ☆ ☆ ☆

Tomorrow morning will be even better because _____

_____

_____

_____

_____

_____

There's nothing like deep breaths after laughing that hard. Nothing in the world like a sore stomach for the right reasons.

STEPHEN CHBOSKY,
American author

Date / /

THIS MORNING, I FEEL				AT THE END OF TODAY, I WANT TO FEEL			
	slightly		very		slightly		very
Calm				Productive			
Rested				Happy			
Cheerful				Fulfilled			
Confident				Inspired			
Focused				Free			
Tired				Relaxed			
Emotional				Strong			
Stressed				In control			
Overwhelmed				Content			
Angry				Relieved			

This morning, I feel _____ because _____

_____

To feel _____ at the end of the day, I will choose to prioritize

1 _____

2 _____

3 _____

To honor my priorities, I will

1 _____

2 _____

3 _____

Three things I want to accomplish today

1 _____

2 _____

3 _____

To complete these goals, I will

1 _____

2 _____

3 _____

THIS IS HOW I PLAN TO USE MY TIME TODAY

5 AM	
6 AM	
7 AM	
8 AM	
9 AM	
10 AM	
11 AM	
12 PM	
1 PM	
2 PM	
3 PM	
4 PM	
5 PM	
6 PM	
7 PM	
8 PM	
9 PM	
10 PM	
11 PM	
12 AM	

I give today ☆ ☆ ☆ ☆ ☆

Tomorrow morning will be even better because _____

_____

_____

_____

_____

Happiness is not a goal...it's a by-product of a life well lived.

ELEANOR ROOSEVELT,
*thirty-second first lady
of the United States*

Date / /

THIS MORNING, I FEEL		slightly			very		AT THE END OF TODAY, I WANT TO FEEL		slightly			very
Calm							Productive					
Rested							Happy					
Cheerful							Fulfilled					
Confident							Inspired					
Focused							Free					
Tired							Relaxed					
Emotional							Strong					
Stressed							In control					
Overwhelmed							Content					
Angry							Relieved					

This morning, I feel _____ because _____
_____

To feel _____ at the end of the day, I will choose to prioritize

1 _____

2 _____

3 _____

Three things I want to accomplish today

1 _____

2 _____

3 _____

To honor my priorities, I will

1 _____

2 _____

3 _____

To complete these goals, I will

1 _____

2 _____

3 _____

THIS IS HOW I PLAN TO USE MY TIME TODAY

5 AM	
6 AM	
7 AM	
8 AM	
9 AM	
10 AM	
11 AM	
12 PM	
1 PM	
2 PM	
3 PM	
4 PM	
5 PM	
6 PM	
7 PM	
8 PM	
9 PM	
10 PM	
11 PM	
12 AM	

I give today ☆ ☆ ☆ ☆ ☆

Tomorrow morning will be
even better because _____

_____

_____

_____

_____

_____

*Dream as if
you'll live forever,
live as if you'll
die today.*

JAMES DEAN,
American actor

Date / /

THIS MORNING, I FEEL						AT THE END OF TODAY, I WANT TO FEEL					
	slightly			very			slightly			very	
Calm						Productive					
Rested						Happy					
Cheerful						Fulfilled					
Confident						Inspired					
Focused						Free					
Tired						Relaxed					
Emotional						Strong					
Stressed						In control					
Overwhelmed						Content					
Angry						Relieved					

This morning, I feel _____ because _____

_____

To feel _____ at the end of the day, I will choose to prioritize

1 _____

2 _____

3 _____

To honor my priorities, I will

1 _____

2 _____

3 _____

Three things I want to accomplish today

1 _____

2 _____

3 _____

To complete these goals, I will

1 _____

2 _____

3 _____

THIS IS HOW I PLAN TO USE MY TIME TODAY

5 AM	
6 AM	
7 AM	
8 AM	
9 AM	
10 AM	
11 AM	
12 PM	
1 PM	
2 PM	
3 PM	
4 PM	
5 PM	
6 PM	
7 PM	
8 PM	
9 PM	
10 PM	
11 PM	
12 AM	

I give today ☆ ☆ ☆ ☆ ☆

Tomorrow morning will be
even better because _____

_____

_____

_____

_____

_____

*If you want
the rainbow,
you gotta put
up with the rain.*

DOLLY PARTON,
*American singer and
songwriter*

Date / /

THIS MORNING, I FEEL						AT THE END OF TODAY, I WANT TO FEEL					
	slightly			very			slightly			very	
Calm						Productive					
Rested						Happy					
Cheerful						Fulfilled					
Confident						Inspired					
Focused						Free					
Tired						Relaxed					
Emotional						Strong					
Stressed						In control					
Overwhelmed						Content					
Angry						Relieved					

This morning, I feel _____ because _____
_____

To feel _____ at the end of the day, I will choose to prioritize

1 _____
2 _____
3 _____

To honor my priorities, I will

1 _____
2 _____
3 _____

Three things I want to accomplish today

1 _____
2 _____
3 _____

To complete these goals, I will

1 _____
2 _____
3 _____

THIS IS HOW I PLAN TO USE MY TIME TODAY

5 AM	
6 AM	
7 AM	
8 AM	
9 AM	
10 AM	
11 AM	
12 PM	
1 PM	
2 PM	
3 PM	
4 PM	
5 PM	
6 PM	
7 PM	
8 PM	
9 PM	
10 PM	
11 PM	
12 AM	

I give today ☆ ☆ ☆ ☆ ☆

Tomorrow morning will be even better because _____

_____

_____

_____

_____

_____

Let us be grateful to the people who make us happy; they are the charming gardeners who make our souls blossom.

MARCEL PROUST,
French author

Date / /

THIS MORNING, I FEEL						AT THE END OF TODAY, I WANT TO FEEL					
	slightly			very			slightly			very	
Calm						Productive					
Rested						Happy					
Cheerful						Fulfilled					
Confident						Inspired					
Focused						Free					
Tired						Relaxed					
Emotional						Strong					
Stressed						In control					
Overwhelmed						Content					
Angry						Relieved					

This morning, I feel _____ because _____

_____

To feel _____ at the end of the day, I will choose to prioritize

1 _____

2 _____

3 _____

To honor my priorities, I will

1 _____

2 _____

3 _____

Three things I want to accomplish today

1 _____

2 _____

3 _____

To complete these goals, I will

1 _____

2 _____

3 _____

THIS IS HOW I PLAN TO USE MY TIME TODAY

5 AM	
6 AM	
7 AM	
8 AM	
9 AM	
10 AM	
11 AM	
12 PM	
1 PM	
2 PM	
3 PM	
4 PM	
5 PM	
6 PM	
7 PM	
8 PM	
9 PM	
10 PM	
11 PM	
12 AM	

I give today ☆ ☆ ☆ ☆ ☆

Tomorrow morning will be even better because _____

_____

_____

_____

_____

_____

_____

Success is getting what you want. Happiness is wanting what you get.

DALE CARNEGIE,
American author

Date   /   /

THIS MORNING, I FEEL	slightly		very		AT THE END OF TODAY, I WANT TO FEEL	slightly		very	
Calm					Productive				
Rested					Happy				
Cheerful					Fulfilled				
Confident					Inspired				
Focused					Free				
Tired					Relaxed				
Emotional					Strong				
Stressed					In control				
Overwhelmed					Content				
Angry					Relieved				

This morning, I feel _____ because _____

_____

To feel _____ at the end of
the day, I will choose to prioritize

1 _____

2 _____

3 _____

Three things I want to accomplish
today

1 _____

2 _____

3 _____

To honor my priorities, I will

1 _____

2 _____

3 _____

To complete these goals, I will

1 _____

2 _____

3 _____

THIS IS HOW I PLAN TO USE MY TIME TODAY

5 AM	
6 AM	
7 AM	
8 AM	
9 AM	
10 AM	
11 AM	
12 PM	
1 PM	
2 PM	
3 PM	
4 PM	
5 PM	
6 PM	
7 PM	
8 PM	
9 PM	
10 PM	
11 PM	
12 AM	

I give today ☆ ☆ ☆ ☆ ☆

Tomorrow morning will be even better because _____

_____

_____

_____

_____

The best way to cheer yourself is to try to cheer somebody else up.

MARK TWAIN,
American author

Date / /

THIS MORNING, I FEEL		slightly			very		AT THE END OF TODAY, I WANT TO FEEL		slightly			very	
Calm							Productive						
Rested							Happy						
Cheerful							Fulfilled						
Confident							Inspired						
Focused							Free						
Tired							Relaxed						
Emotional							Strong						
Stressed							In control						
Overwhelmed							Content						
Angry							Relieved						

This morning, I feel _____ because _____

To feel _____ at the end of the day, I will choose to prioritize

1 _____
2 _____
3 _____

To honor my priorities, I will

1 _____
2 _____
3 _____

Three things I want to accomplish today

1 _____
2 _____
3 _____

To complete these goals, I will

1 _____
2 _____
3 _____

THIS IS HOW I PLAN TO USE MY TIME TODAY

5 AM	
6 AM	
7 AM	
8 AM	
9 AM	
10 AM	
11 AM	
12 PM	
1 PM	
2 PM	
3 PM	
4 PM	
5 PM	
6 PM	
7 PM	
8 PM	
9 PM	
10 PM	
11 PM	
12 AM	

I give today ☆ ☆ ☆ ☆ ☆

Tomorrow morning will be
even better because _____

_____

_____

_____

_____

_____

It was only a sunny smile, and little it cost in the giving, but like morning light it scattered the night and made the day worth living.

F. SCOTT FITZGERALD,
American author

Date / /

THIS MORNING, I FEEL						
	slightly				very	
Calm						
Rested						
Cheerful						
Confident						
Focused						
Tired						
Emotional						
Stressed						
Overwhelmed						
Angry						

AT THE END OF TODAY, I WANT TO FEEL						
	slightly				very	
Productive						
Happy						
Fulfilled						
Inspired						
Free						
Relaxed						
Strong						
In control						
Content						
Relieved						

This morning, I feel _____ because _____

_____

To feel _____ at the end of the day, I will choose to prioritize

1 _____

2 _____

3 _____

Three things I want to accomplish today

1 _____

2 _____

3 _____

To honor my priorities, I will

1 _____

2 _____

3 _____

To complete these goals, I will

1 _____

2 _____

3 _____

THIS IS HOW I PLAN TO USE MY TIME TODAY

5 AM	
6 AM	
7 AM	
8 AM	
9 AM	
10 AM	
11 AM	
12 PM	
1 PM	
2 PM	
3 PM	
4 PM	
5 PM	
6 PM	
7 PM	
8 PM	
9 PM	
10 PM	
11 PM	
12 AM	

I give today ☆ ☆ ☆ ☆ ☆

Tomorrow morning will be
even better because _____

_____

_____

_____

_____

_____

*Those who are not
looking for happiness
are the most likely to find
it, because those who are
searching forget that the
surest way to be happy is to
seek happiness for others.*

MARTIN LUTHER KING JR.,
American civil rights leader

Date / /

THIS MORNING, I FEEL			AT THE END OF TODAY, I WANT TO FEEL		
	slightly	very		slightly	very
Calm			Productive		
Rested			Happy		
Cheerful			Fulfilled		
Confident			Inspired		
Focused			Free		
Tired			Relaxed		
Emotional			Strong		
Stressed			In control		
Overwhelmed			Content		
Angry			Relieved		

This morning, I feel _____ because _____

_____

To feel _____ at the end of
the day, I will choose to prioritize

1 _____

2 _____

3 _____

Three things I want to accomplish
today

1 _____

2 _____

3 _____

To honor my priorities, I will

1 _____

2 _____

3 _____

To complete these goals, I will

1 _____

2 _____

3 _____

THIS IS HOW I PLAN TO USE MY TIME TODAY

5 AM	
6 AM	
7 AM	
8 AM	
9 AM	
10 AM	
11 AM	
12 PM	
1 PM	
2 PM	
3 PM	
4 PM	
5 PM	
6 PM	
7 PM	
8 PM	
9 PM	
10 PM	
11 PM	
12 AM	

I give today ☆ ☆ ☆ ☆ ☆

Tomorrow morning will be even better because _____

_____

_____

_____

_____

_____

I think happiness is what makes you pretty. Period. Happy people are beautiful. They become like a mirror and they reflect that happiness.

DREW BARRYMORE,
American actor

Date / /

THIS MORNING, I FEEL	slightly				very		AT THE END OF TODAY, I WANT TO FEEL	slightly				very	
Calm							Productive						
Rested							Happy						
Cheerful							Fulfilled						
Confident							Inspired						
Focused							Free						
Tired							Relaxed						
Emotional							Strong						
Stressed							In control						
Overwhelmed							Content						
Angry							Relieved						

This morning, I feel _____ because _____

_____

To feel _____ at the end of the day, I will choose to prioritize

1 _____
2 _____
3 _____

Three things I want to accomplish today

1 _____
2 _____
3 _____

To honor my priorities, I will

1 _____
2 _____
3 _____

To complete these goals, I will

1 _____
2 _____
3 _____

THIS IS HOW I PLAN TO USE MY TIME TODAY

5 AM	
6 AM	
7 AM	
8 AM	
9 AM	
10 AM	
11 AM	
12 PM	
1 PM	
2 PM	
3 PM	
4 PM	
5 PM	
6 PM	
7 PM	
8 PM	
9 PM	
10 PM	
11 PM	
12 AM	

I give today ☆ ☆ ☆ ☆ ☆

Tomorrow morning will be even better because _____

_____

_____

_____

_____

_____

_____

It is not how much we have, but how much we enjoy, that makes happiness.

CHARLES SPURGEON,
nineteenth-century English preacher and author

Date / /

THIS MORNING, I FEEL						AT THE END OF TODAY, I WANT TO FEEL					
	slightly			very			slightly			very	
Calm						Productive					
Rested						Happy					
Cheerful						Fulfilled					
Confident						Inspired					
Focused						Free					
Tired						Relaxed					
Emotional						Strong					
Stressed						In control					
Overwhelmed						Content					
Angry						Relieved					

This morning, I feel _____ because _____

_____

To feel _____ at the end of
the day, I will choose to prioritize

1 _____

2 _____

3 _____

Three things I want to accomplish
today

1 _____

2 _____

3 _____

To honor my priorities, I will

1 _____

2 _____

3 _____

To complete these goals, I will

1 _____

2 _____

3 _____

THIS IS HOW I PLAN TO USE MY TIME TODAY

5 AM	
6 AM	
7 AM	
8 AM	
9 AM	
10 AM	
11 AM	
12 PM	
1 PM	
2 PM	
3 PM	
4 PM	
5 PM	
6 PM	
7 PM	
8 PM	
9 PM	
10 PM	
11 PM	
12 AM	

I give today ☆ ☆ ☆ ☆ ☆

Tomorrow morning will be
even better because _____

_____

_____

_____

_____

_____

_____

*If you spend
your whole life
waiting for the
storm, you'll
never enjoy the
sunshine.*

MORRIS WEST,
Australian author

Date / /

THIS MORNING, I FEEL						AT THE END OF TODAY, I WANT TO FEEL					
	slightly			very			slightly			very	
Calm						Productive					
Rested						Happy					
Cheerful						Fulfilled					
Confident						Inspired					
Focused						Free					
Tired						Relaxed					
Emotional						Strong					
Stressed						In control					
Overwhelmed						Content					
Angry						Relieved					

This morning, I feel _____ because _____

_____

To feel _____ at the end of
the day, I will choose to prioritize

1 _____

2 _____

3 _____

To honor my priorities, I will

1 _____

2 _____

3 _____

Three things I want to accomplish
today

1 _____

2 _____

3 _____

To complete these goals, I will

1 _____

2 _____

3 _____

THIS IS HOW I PLAN TO USE MY TIME TODAY

5 AM	
6 AM	
7 AM	
8 AM	
9 AM	
10 AM	
11 AM	
12 PM	
1 PM	
2 PM	
3 PM	
4 PM	
5 PM	
6 PM	
7 PM	
8 PM	
9 PM	
10 PM	
11 PM	
12 AM	

I give today ☆ ☆ ☆ ☆ ☆

Tomorrow morning will be even better because _____

_____

_____

_____

_____

_____

It's the moments that I stopped just to be, rather than do, that have given me true happiness.

RICHARD BRANSON,
English entrepreneur

Date / /

THIS MORNING, I FEEL							AT THE END OF TODAY, I WANT TO FEEL						
	slightly			very				slightly			very		
Calm							Productive						
Rested							Happy						
Cheerful							Fulfilled						
Confident							Inspired						
Focused							Free						
Tired							Relaxed						
Emotional							Strong						
Stressed							In control						
Overwhelmed							Content						
Angry							Relieved						

This morning, I feel _____ because _____

_____

To feel _____ at the end of
the day, I will choose to prioritize

1 _____

2 _____

3 _____

Three things I want to accomplish
today

1 _____

2 _____

3 _____

To honor my priorities, I will

1 _____

2 _____

3 _____

To complete these goals, I will

1 _____

2 _____

3 _____

THIS IS HOW I PLAN TO USE MY TIME TODAY

5 AM	
6 AM	
7 AM	
8 AM	
9 AM	
10 AM	
11 AM	
12 PM	
1 PM	
2 PM	
3 PM	
4 PM	
5 PM	
6 PM	
7 PM	
8 PM	
9 PM	
10 PM	
11 PM	
12 AM	

I give today ☆ ☆ ☆ ☆ ☆

Tomorrow morning will be even better because _____

_____

_____

_____

_____

_____

"What day is it?"
asked Winnie the Pooh.

"It's today,"
squeaked Piglet.

"My favorite day,"
said Pooh.

A.A. MILNE,
English author

Date   /   /

THIS MORNING, I FEEL						AT THE END OF TODAY, I WANT TO FEEL					
	slightly			very			slightly			very	
Calm						Productive					
Rested						Happy					
Cheerful						Fulfilled					
Confident						Inspired					
Focused						Free					
Tired						Relaxed					
Emotional						Strong					
Stressed						In control					
Overwhelmed						Content					
Angry						Relieved					

This morning, I feel _____ because _____

_____

To feel _____ at the end of the day, I will choose to prioritize

1 _____

2 _____

3 _____

To honor my priorities, I will

1 _____

2 _____

3 _____

Three things I want to accomplish today

1 _____

2 _____

3 _____

To complete these goals, I will

1 _____

2 _____

3 _____

THIS IS HOW I PLAN TO USE MY TIME TODAY

5 AM	
6 AM	
7 AM	
8 AM	
9 AM	
10 AM	
11 AM	
12 PM	
1 PM	
2 PM	
3 PM	
4 PM	
5 PM	
6 PM	
7 PM	
8 PM	
9 PM	
10 PM	
11 PM	
12 AM	

I give today ☆ ☆ ☆ ☆ ☆

Tomorrow morning will be even better because _____

_____

_____

_____

_____

_____

Everyone wants to live on top of the mountain, but all the happiness and growth occurs while you're climbing it.

ANDY ROONEY,
American radio and TV writer

Date / /

THIS MORNING, I FEEL	slightly			very	
Calm					
Rested					
Cheerful					
Confident					
Focused					
Tired					
Emotional					
Stressed					
Overwhelmed					
Angry					

AT THE END OF TODAY, I WANT TO FEEL	slightly			very	
Productive					
Happy					
Fulfilled					
Inspired					
Free					
Relaxed					
Strong					
In control					
Content					
Relieved					

This morning, I feel _____ because _____

_____

To feel _____ at the end of the day, I will choose to prioritize

1 _____

2 _____

3 _____

To honor my priorities, I will

1 _____

2 _____

3 _____

Three things I want to accomplish today

1 _____

2 _____

3 _____

To complete these goals, I will

1 _____

2 _____

3 _____

THIS IS HOW I PLAN TO USE MY TIME TODAY

5 AM	
6 AM	
7 AM	
8 AM	
9 AM	
10 AM	
11 AM	
12 PM	
1 PM	
2 PM	
3 PM	
4 PM	
5 PM	
6 PM	
7 PM	
8 PM	
9 PM	
10 PM	
11 PM	
12 AM	

I give today ☆ ☆ ☆ ☆ ☆

Tomorrow morning will be even better because _____

_____

_____

_____

_____

_____

Optimism is a happiness magnet. If you stay positive, good things and good people will be drawn to you.

MARY LOU RETTON,
American gymnast

Date / /

THIS MORNING, I FEEL						AT THE END OF TODAY, I WANT TO FEEL					
	slightly			very			slightly			very	
Calm						Productive					
Rested						Happy					
Cheerful						Fulfilled					
Confident						Inspired					
Focused						Free					
Tired						Relaxed					
Emotional						Strong					
Stressed						In control					
Overwhelmed						Content					
Angry						Relieved					

This morning, I feel _____ because _____

_____

To feel _____ at the end of the day, I will choose to prioritize

1 _____
2 _____
3 _____

Three things I want to accomplish today

1 _____
2 _____
3 _____

To honor my priorities, I will

1 _____
2 _____
3 _____

To complete these goals, I will

1 _____
2 _____
3 _____

THIS IS HOW I PLAN TO USE MY TIME TODAY

5 AM	
6 AM	
7 AM	
8 AM	
9 AM	
10 AM	
11 AM	
12 PM	
1 PM	
2 PM	
3 PM	
4 PM	
5 PM	
6 PM	
7 PM	
8 PM	
9 PM	
10 PM	
11 PM	
12 AM	

I give today ☆ ☆ ☆ ☆ ☆

Tomorrow morning will be
even better because _____

_____

_____

_____

_____

_____

*Even the darkest
night will end and
the sun will rise.*

VICTOR HUGO,
*French poet, author,
and playwright*

Date / /

THIS MORNING, I FEEL						AT THE END OF TODAY, I WANT TO FEEL					
	slightly			very			slightly			very	
Calm						Productive					
Rested						Happy					
Cheerful						Fulfilled					
Confident						Inspired					
Focused						Free					
Tired						Relaxed					
Emotional						Strong					
Stressed						In control					
Overwhelmed						Content					
Angry						Relieved					

This morning, I feel _____ because _____

_____

To feel _____ at the end of
the day, I will choose to prioritize

1 _____

2 _____

3 _____

To honor my priorities, I will

1 _____

2 _____

3 _____

Three things I want to accomplish
today

1 _____

2 _____

3 _____

To complete these goals, I will

1 _____

2 _____

3 _____

THIS IS HOW I PLAN TO USE MY TIME TODAY

5 AM	
6 AM	
7 AM	
8 AM	
9 AM	
10 AM	
11 AM	
12 PM	
1 PM	
2 PM	
3 PM	
4 PM	
5 PM	
6 PM	
7 PM	
8 PM	
9 PM	
10 PM	
11 PM	
12 AM	

I give today ☆ ☆ ☆ ☆ ☆

Tomorrow morning will be even better because _____

_____

_____

_____

_____

_____

People become attached to their burdens sometimes more than the burdens are attached to them.

GEORGE BERNARD SHAW,
Irish playwright

Date / /

THIS MORNING, I FEEL				slightly			very	AT THE END OF TODAY, I WANT TO FEEL				slightly			very
Calm								Productive							
Rested								Happy							
Cheerful								Fulfilled							
Confident								Inspired							
Focused								Free							
Tired								Relaxed							
Emotional								Strong							
Stressed								In control							
Overwhelmed								Content							
Angry								Relieved							

This morning, I feel _____ because _____

_____

To feel _____ at the end of the day, I will choose to prioritize

1 _____

2 _____

3 _____

To honor my priorities, I will

1 _____

2 _____

3 _____

Three things I want to accomplish today

1 _____

2 _____

3 _____

To complete these goals, I will

1 _____

2 _____

3 _____

THIS IS HOW I PLAN TO USE MY TIME TODAY

5 AM	
6 AM	
7 AM	
8 AM	
9 AM	
10 AM	
11 AM	
12 PM	
1 PM	
2 PM	
3 PM	
4 PM	
5 PM	
6 PM	
7 PM	
8 PM	
9 PM	
10 PM	
11 PM	
12 AM	

I give today ☆ ☆ ☆ ☆ ☆

Tomorrow morning will be
even better because _____

_____

_____

_____

_____

_____

*Even the tallest trees
are able to grow from
tiny seeds like these.
Remember this, and
try not to rush time.*

PAULO COELHO,
*Brazilian lyricist
and author*

Date / /

THIS MORNING, I FEEL						AT THE END OF TODAY, I WANT TO FEEL					
	slightly			very			slightly			very	
Calm						Productive					
Rested						Happy					
Cheerful						Fulfilled					
Confident						Inspired					
Focused						Free					
Tired						Relaxed					
Emotional						Strong					
Stressed						In control					
Overwhelmed						Content					
Angry						Relieved					

This morning, I feel _____ because _____

_____

To feel _____ at the end of
the day, I will choose to prioritize

1 _____

2 _____

3 _____

Three things I want to accomplish
today

1 _____

2 _____

3 _____

To honor my priorities, I will

1 _____

2 _____

3 _____

To complete these goals, I will

1 _____

2 _____

3 _____

THIS IS HOW I PLAN TO USE MY TIME TODAY

5 AM	
6 AM	
7 AM	
8 AM	
9 AM	
10 AM	
11 AM	
12 PM	
1 PM	
2 PM	
3 PM	
4 PM	
5 PM	
6 PM	
7 PM	
8 PM	
9 PM	
10 PM	
11 PM	
12 AM	

I give today ☆ ☆ ☆ ☆ ☆

Tomorrow morning will be
even better because _____

_____

_____

_____

_____

_____

*If we learn to open
our hearts, anyone,
including the people
who drive us crazy,
can be our teacher.*

PEMA CHÖDRÖN,
*American Buddhist nun,
teacher, and author*

Date / /

THIS MORNING, I FEEL						AT THE END OF TODAY, I WANT TO FEEL					
	slightly				very		slightly				very
Calm						Productive					
Rested						Happy					
Cheerful						Fulfilled					
Confident						Inspired					
Focused						Free					
Tired						Relaxed					
Emotional						Strong					
Stressed						In control					
Overwhelmed						Content					
Angry						Relieved					

This morning, I feel _____ because _____

_____

To feel _____ at the end of
the day, I will choose to prioritize

1 _____

2 _____

3 _____

Three things I want to accomplish
today

1 _____

2 _____

3 _____

To honor my priorities, I will

1 _____

2 _____

3 _____

To complete these goals, I will

1 _____

2 _____

3 _____

THIS IS HOW I PLAN TO USE MY TIME TODAY

5 AM	
6 AM	
7 AM	
8 AM	
9 AM	
10 AM	
11 AM	
12 PM	
1 PM	
2 PM	
3 PM	
4 PM	
5 PM	
6 PM	
7 PM	
8 PM	
9 PM	
10 PM	
11 PM	
12 AM	

I give today ☆ ☆ ☆ ☆ ☆

Tomorrow morning will be even better because _____

_____

_____

_____

_____

_____

Everything we do is infused with the energy with which we do it. If we're frantic, life will be frantic. If we're peaceful, life will be peaceful.

MARIANNE WILLIAMSON,
American spiritual teacher, author, and lecturer

Date / /

THIS MORNING, I FEEL						AT THE END OF TODAY, I WANT TO FEEL					
	slightly			very			slightly			very	
Calm						Productive					
Rested						Happy					
Cheerful						Fulfilled					
Confident						Inspired					
Focused						Free					
Tired						Relaxed					
Emotional						Strong					
Stressed						In control					
Overwhelmed						Content					
Angry						Relieved					

This morning, I feel _____ because _____

_____

To feel _____ at the end of the day, I will choose to prioritize

1 _____
2 _____
3 _____

Three things I want to accomplish today

1 _____
2 _____
3 _____

To honor my priorities, I will

1 _____
2 _____
3 _____

To complete these goals, I will

1 _____
2 _____
3 _____

THIS IS HOW I PLAN TO USE MY TIME TODAY

5 AM	
6 AM	
7 AM	
8 AM	
9 AM	
10 AM	
11 AM	
12 PM	
1 PM	
2 PM	
3 PM	
4 PM	
5 PM	
6 PM	
7 PM	
8 PM	
9 PM	
10 PM	
11 PM	
12 AM	

I give today ☆ ☆ ☆ ☆ ☆

Tomorrow morning will be even better because _____

_____

_____

_____

_____

_____

Nothing can bring you peace but yourself.

RALPH WALDO EMERSON,
American philosopher and poet

Date / /

THIS MORNING, I FEEL				AT THE END OF TODAY, I WANT TO FEEL			
	slightly		very		slightly		very
Calm				Productive			
Rested				Happy			
Cheerful				Fulfilled			
Confident				Inspired			
Focused				Free			
Tired				Relaxed			
Emotional				Strong			
Stressed				In control			
Overwhelmed				Content			
Angry				Relieved			

This morning, I feel _____ because _____

_____

To feel _____ at the end of the day, I will choose to prioritize

1 _____

2 _____

3 _____

To honor my priorities, I will

1 _____

2 _____

3 _____

Three things I want to accomplish today

1 _____

2 _____

3 _____

To complete these goals, I will

1 _____

2 _____

3 _____

THIS IS HOW I PLAN TO USE MY TIME TODAY

5 AM	
6 AM	
7 AM	
8 AM	
9 AM	
10 AM	
11 AM	
12 PM	
1 PM	
2 PM	
3 PM	
4 PM	
5 PM	
6 PM	
7 PM	
8 PM	
9 PM	
10 PM	
11 PM	
12 AM	

I give today ☆ ☆ ☆ ☆ ☆

Tomorrow morning will be even better because _____

_____

_____

_____

_____

Anxiety does not empty tomorrow of its sorrows, but only empties today of its strength.

CHARLES SPURGEON,
nineteenth-century English preacher and author

Date / /

THIS MORNING, I FEEL					AT THE END OF TODAY, I WANT TO FEEL				
	slightly			very		slightly			very
Calm					Productive				
Rested					Happy				
Cheerful					Fulfilled				
Confident					Inspired				
Focused					Free				
Tired					Relaxed				
Emotional					Strong				
Stressed					In control				
Overwhelmed					Content				
Angry					Relieved				

This morning, I feel _____ because _____

_____

To feel _____ at the end of
the day, I will choose to prioritize

1 _____

2 _____

3 _____

Three things I want to accomplish
today

1 _____

2 _____

3 _____

To honor my priorities, I will

1 _____

2 _____

3 _____

To complete these goals, I will

1 _____

2 _____

3 _____

THIS IS HOW I PLAN TO USE MY TIME TODAY

5 AM	
6 AM	
7 AM	
8 AM	
9 AM	
10 AM	
11 AM	
12 PM	
1 PM	
2 PM	
3 PM	
4 PM	
5 PM	
6 PM	
7 PM	
8 PM	
9 PM	
10 PM	
11 PM	
12 AM	

I give today ☆ ☆ ☆ ☆ ☆

Tomorrow morning will be even better because _____

_____

_____

_____

_____

_____

No need to hurry. No need to sparkle. No need to be anybody but oneself.

VIRGINIA WOOLF,
English author

Date / /

THIS MORNING, I FEEL						AT THE END OF TODAY, I WANT TO FEEL					
	slightly			very			slightly			very	
Calm						Productive					
Rested						Happy					
Cheerful						Fulfilled					
Confident						Inspired					
Focused						Free					
Tired						Relaxed					
Emotional						Strong					
Stressed						In control					
Overwhelmed						Content					
Angry						Relieved					

This morning, I feel _____ because _____

_____

To feel _____ at the end of the day, I will choose to prioritize

1 _____

2 _____

3 _____

To honor my priorities, I will

1 _____

2 _____

3 _____

Three things I want to accomplish today

1 _____

2 _____

3 _____

To complete these goals, I will

1 _____

2 _____

3 _____

THIS IS HOW I PLAN TO USE MY TIME TODAY

5 AM	
6 AM	
7 AM	
8 AM	
9 AM	
10 AM	
11 AM	
12 PM	
1 PM	
2 PM	
3 PM	
4 PM	
5 PM	
6 PM	
7 PM	
8 PM	
9 PM	
10 PM	
11 PM	
12 AM	

I give today ☆ ☆ ☆ ☆ ☆

Tomorrow morning will be
even better because _____

_____

_____

_____

_____

_____

For fast-acting relief, try slowing down.

LILY TOMLIN,
American actor

Date / /

THIS MORNING, I FEEL						AT THE END OF TODAY, I WANT TO FEEL					
	slightly			very			slightly			very	
Calm						Productive					
Rested						Happy					
Cheerful						Fulfilled					
Confident						Inspired					
Focused						Free					
Tired						Relaxed					
Emotional						Strong					
Stressed						In control					
Overwhelmed						Content					
Angry						Relieved					

This morning, I feel _____ because _____

_____

To feel _____ at the end of the day, I will choose to prioritize

1 _____

2 _____

3 _____

Three things I want to accomplish today

1 _____

2 _____

3 _____

To honor my priorities, I will

1 _____

2 _____

3 _____

To complete these goals, I will

1 _____

2 _____

3 _____

THIS IS HOW I PLAN TO USE MY TIME TODAY

5 AM	
6 AM	
7 AM	
8 AM	
9 AM	
10 AM	
11 AM	
12 PM	
1 PM	
2 PM	
3 PM	
4 PM	
5 PM	
6 PM	
7 PM	
8 PM	
9 PM	
10 PM	
11 PM	
12 AM	

I give today ☆ ☆ ☆ ☆ ☆

Tomorrow morning will be even better because _____

_____

_____

_____

_____

_____

Anxiety's like a rocking chair. It gives you something to do, but it doesn't get you very far.

JODI PICOULT,
American author

Date / /

THIS MORNING, I FEEL						AT THE END OF TODAY, I WANT TO FEEL					
	slightly			very			slightly			very	
Calm						Productive					
Rested						Happy					
Cheerful						Fulfilled					
Confident						Inspired					
Focused						Free					
Tired						Relaxed					
Emotional						Strong					
Stressed						In control					
Overwhelmed						Content					
Angry						Relieved					

This morning, I feel _____ because _____

_____

To feel _____ at the end of
the day, I will choose to prioritize

1 _____

2 _____

3 _____

Three things I want to accomplish
today

1 _____

2 _____

3 _____

To honor my priorities, I will

1 _____

2 _____

3 _____

To complete these goals, I will

1 _____

2 _____

3 _____

THIS IS HOW I PLAN TO USE MY TIME TODAY

5 AM	
6 AM	
7 AM	
8 AM	
9 AM	
10 AM	
11 AM	
12 PM	
1 PM	
2 PM	
3 PM	
4 PM	
5 PM	
6 PM	
7 PM	
8 PM	
9 PM	
10 PM	
11 PM	
12 AM	

I give today ☆ ☆ ☆ ☆ ☆

Tomorrow morning will be
even better because _____

_____

_____

_____

_____

_____

*Just one small
positive thought
in the morning
can change your
whole day.*

TENZIN GYATSO,
*His Holiness the
Fourteenth Dalai Lama*

Date / /

THIS MORNING, I FEEL							AT THE END OF TODAY, I WANT TO FEEL						
	slightly			very				slightly			very		
Calm							Productive						
Rested							Happy						
Cheerful							Fulfilled						
Confident							Inspired						
Focused							Free						
Tired							Relaxed						
Emotional							Strong						
Stressed							In control						
Overwhelmed							Content						
Angry							Relieved						

This morning, I feel _____ because _____

_____

To feel _____ at the end of the day, I will choose to prioritize

1 _____

2 _____

3 _____

Three things I want to accomplish today

1 _____

2 _____

3 _____

To honor my priorities, I will

1 _____

2 _____

3 _____

To complete these goals, I will

1 _____

2 _____

3 _____

THIS IS HOW I PLAN TO USE MY TIME TODAY

5 AM	
6 AM	
7 AM	
8 AM	
9 AM	
10 AM	
11 AM	
12 PM	
1 PM	
2 PM	
3 PM	
4 PM	
5 PM	
6 PM	
7 PM	
8 PM	
9 PM	
10 PM	
11 PM	
12 AM	

I give today ☆ ☆ ☆ ☆ ☆

Tomorrow morning will be even better because _____

_____

_____

_____

_____

_____

The most important relationship in your life is the relationship you have with yourself. Because no matter what happens, you will always be with yourself.

DIANE VON FÜRSTENBERG,
Belgian fashion designer

Date / /

THIS MORNING, I FEEL						AT THE END OF TODAY, I WANT TO FEEL					
	slightly			very			slightly			very	
Calm						Productive					
Rested						Happy					
Cheerful						Fulfilled					
Confident						Inspired					
Focused						Free					
Tired						Relaxed					
Emotional						Strong					
Stressed						In control					
Overwhelmed						Content					
Angry						Relieved					

This morning, I feel _____ because _____

_____

To feel _____ at the end of the day, I will choose to prioritize

1 _____

2 _____

3 _____

To honor my priorities, I will

1 _____

2 _____

3 _____

Three things I want to accomplish today

1 _____

2 _____

3 _____

To complete these goals, I will

1 _____

2 _____

3 _____

THIS IS HOW I PLAN TO USE MY TIME TODAY

5 AM	
6 AM	
7 AM	
8 AM	
9 AM	
10 AM	
11 AM	
12 PM	
1 PM	
2 PM	
3 PM	
4 PM	
5 PM	
6 PM	
7 PM	
8 PM	
9 PM	
10 PM	
11 PM	
12 AM	

I give today ☆ ☆ ☆ ☆ ☆

Tomorrow morning will be even better because _____

_____

_____

_____

_____

_____

Almost everything will work again if you unplug it for a few minutes, including you.

ANNE LAMOTT,
American author

Date / /

THIS MORNING, I FEEL		slightly				very		AT THE END OF TODAY, I WANT TO FEEL		slightly				very
Calm								Productive						
Rested								Happy						
Cheerful								Fulfilled						
Confident								Inspired						
Focused								Free						
Tired								Relaxed						
Emotional								Strong						
Stressed								In control						
Overwhelmed								Content						
Angry								Relieved						

This morning, I feel _____ because _____

_____

To feel _____ at the end of the day, I will choose to prioritize

1 _____

2 _____

3 _____

Three things I want to accomplish today

1 _____

2 _____

3 _____

To honor my priorities, I will

1 _____

2 _____

3 _____

To complete these goals, I will

1 _____

2 _____

3 _____

THIS IS HOW I PLAN TO USE MY TIME TODAY

5 AM	
6 AM	
7 AM	
8 AM	
9 AM	
10 AM	
11 AM	
12 PM	
1 PM	
2 PM	
3 PM	
4 PM	
5 PM	
6 PM	
7 PM	
8 PM	
9 PM	
10 PM	
11 PM	
12 AM	

I give today ☆ ☆ ☆ ☆ ☆

Tomorrow morning will be even better because _____

_____

_____

_____

_____

_____

My mission, should I choose to accept it, is to find peace with exactly who and what I am. To take pride in my thoughts, my appearance, my talents, my flaws and to stop this incessant worrying that I can't be loved as I am.

ANAÏS NIN,
Cuban-American author

Date / /

THIS MORNING, I FEEL						AT THE END OF TODAY, I WANT TO FEEL					
	slightly			very			slightly			very	
Calm						Productive					
Rested						Happy					
Cheerful						Fulfilled					
Confident						Inspired					
Focused						Free					
Tired						Relaxed					
Emotional						Strong					
Stressed						In control					
Overwhelmed						Content					
Angry						Relieved					

This morning, I feel _____ because _____

_____

To feel _____ at the end of
the day, I will choose to prioritize

1 _____

2 _____

3 _____

To honor my priorities, I will

1 _____

2 _____

3 _____

Three things I want to accomplish
today

1 _____

2 _____

3 _____

To complete these goals, I will

1 _____

2 _____

3 _____

THIS IS HOW I PLAN TO USE MY TIME TODAY

5 AM	
6 AM	
7 AM	
8 AM	
9 AM	
10 AM	
11 AM	
12 PM	
1 PM	
2 PM	
3 PM	
4 PM	
5 PM	
6 PM	
7 PM	
8 PM	
9 PM	
10 PM	
11 PM	
12 AM	

I give today ☆ ☆ ☆ ☆ ☆

Tomorrow morning will be
even better because _____

_____

_____

_____

_____

_____

*Put blinders on to those
things that conspire to
hold you back, especially
the ones in your own
head. Guard your good
mood. Listen to music
every day, joke, and
love and read more for
fun, especially poetry.*

MERYL STREEP,
American actor

Date / /

THIS MORNING, I FEEL							AT THE END OF TODAY, I WANT TO FEEL						
	slightly			very				slightly			very		
Calm							Productive						
Rested							Happy						
Cheerful							Fulfilled						
Confident							Inspired						
Focused							Free						
Tired							Relaxed						
Emotional							Strong						
Stressed							In control						
Overwhelmed							Content						
Angry							Relieved						

This morning, I feel _____ because _____

_____

To feel _____ at the end of
the day, I will choose to prioritize

1 _____

2 _____

3 _____

Three things I want to accomplish
today

1 _____

2 _____

3 _____

To honor my priorities, I will

1 _____

2 _____

3 _____

To complete these goals, I will

1 _____

2 _____

3 _____

THIS IS HOW I PLAN TO USE MY TIME TODAY

5 AM	
6 AM	
7 AM	
8 AM	
9 AM	
10 AM	
11 AM	
12 PM	
1 PM	
2 PM	
3 PM	
4 PM	
5 PM	
6 PM	
7 PM	
8 PM	
9 PM	
10 PM	
11 PM	
12 AM	

I give today ☆ ☆ ☆ ☆ ☆

Tomorrow morning will be even better because _____

_____

_____

_____

_____

When you recover or discover something that nourishes your soul and brings joy, care enough about yourself to make room for it in your life.

JEAN SHINODA BOLEN, MD,
American psychiatrist
and author

Date / /

THIS MORNING, I FEEL				slightly		very	
Calm							
Rested							
Cheerful							
Confident							
Focused							
Tired							
Emotional							
Stressed							
Overwhelmed							
Angry							

AT THE END OF TODAY, I WANT TO FEEL				slightly		very	
Productive							
Happy							
Fulfilled							
Inspired							
Free							
Relaxed							
Strong							
In control							
Content							
Relieved							

This morning, I feel _____ because _____

_____

To feel _____ at the end of the day, I will choose to prioritize

1 _____

2 _____

3 _____

To honor my priorities, I will

1 _____

2 _____

3 _____

Three things I want to accomplish today

1 _____

2 _____

3 _____

To complete these goals, I will

1 _____

2 _____

3 _____

THIS IS HOW I PLAN TO USE MY TIME TODAY

5 AM	
6 AM	
7 AM	
8 AM	
9 AM	
10 AM	
11 AM	
12 PM	
1 PM	
2 PM	
3 PM	
4 PM	
5 PM	
6 PM	
7 PM	
8 PM	
9 PM	
10 PM	
11 PM	
12 AM	

I give today ☆ ☆ ☆ ☆ ☆

Tomorrow morning will be
even better because _____

_____

_____

_____

_____

_____

*Nourishing
yourself in a way
that helps you blossom
in the direction you
want to go is attainable,
and you are worth
the effort.*

DEBORAH DAY, MA,
*American therapist
and author*

Date / /

THIS MORNING, I FEEL						AT THE END OF TODAY, I WANT TO FEEL					
	slightly			very			slightly			very	
Calm						Productive					
Rested						Happy					
Cheerful						Fulfilled					
Confident						Inspired					
Focused						Free					
Tired						Relaxed					
Emotional						Strong					
Stressed						In control					
Overwhelmed						Content					
Angry						Relieved					

This morning, I feel _____ because _____

_____

To feel _____ at the end of the day, I will choose to prioritize

1 _____

2 _____

3 _____

To honor my priorities, I will

1 _____

2 _____

3 _____

Three things I want to accomplish today

1 _____

2 _____

3 _____

To complete these goals, I will

1 _____

2 _____

3 _____

THIS IS HOW I PLAN TO USE MY TIME TODAY

5 AM	
6 AM	
7 AM	
8 AM	
9 AM	
10 AM	
11 AM	
12 PM	
1 PM	
2 PM	
3 PM	
4 PM	
5 PM	
6 PM	
7 PM	
8 PM	
9 PM	
10 PM	
11 PM	
12 AM	

I give today ☆ ☆ ☆ ☆ ☆

Tomorrow morning will be
even better because _____

_____

_____

_____

_____

_____

*This is a
wonderful day.
I've never seen
this one before.*

MAYA ANGELOU,
*American poet and
author*

Date / /

THIS MORNING, I FEEL							AT THE END OF TODAY, I WANT TO FEEL						
	slightly			very				slightly			very		
Calm							Productive						
Rested							Happy						
Cheerful							Fulfilled						
Confident							Inspired						
Focused							Free						
Tired							Relaxed						
Emotional							Strong						
Stressed							In control						
Overwhelmed							Content						
Angry							Relieved						

This morning, I feel _____ because _____

_____

To feel _____ at the end of the day, I will choose to prioritize

1 _____

2 _____

3 _____

To honor my priorities, I will

1 _____

2 _____

3 _____

Three things I want to accomplish today

1 _____

2 _____

3 _____

To complete these goals, I will

1 _____

2 _____

3 _____

THIS IS HOW I PLAN TO USE MY TIME TODAY

5 AM	
6 AM	
7 AM	
8 AM	
9 AM	
10 AM	
11 AM	
12 PM	
1 PM	
2 PM	
3 PM	
4 PM	
5 PM	
6 PM	
7 PM	
8 PM	
9 PM	
10 PM	
11 PM	
12 AM	

I give today ☆ ☆ ☆ ☆ ☆

Tomorrow morning will be even better because _____

_____

_____

_____

_____

_____

_____

Be thankful for what you have; you'll end up having more. If you concentrate on what you don't have, you will never, ever have enough.

OPRAH WINFREY,
*American entrepreneur,
philanthropist, and
TV host*

Date / /

THIS MORNING, I FEEL	slightly			very	AT THE END OF TODAY, I WANT TO FEEL	slightly			very
Calm					Productive				
Rested					Happy				
Cheerful					Fulfilled				
Confident					Inspired				
Focused					Free				
Tired					Relaxed				
Emotional					Strong				
Stressed					In control				
Overwhelmed					Content				
Angry					Relieved				

This morning, I feel _____ because _____
_____

To feel _____ at the end of the day, I will choose to prioritize

1 _____

2 _____

3 _____

To honor my priorities, I will

1 _____

2 _____

3 _____

Three things I want to accomplish today

1 _____

2 _____

3 _____

To complete these goals, I will

1 _____

2 _____

3 _____

THIS IS HOW I PLAN TO USE MY TIME TODAY

5 AM	
6 AM	
7 AM	
8 AM	
9 AM	
10 AM	
11 AM	
12 PM	
1 PM	
2 PM	
3 PM	
4 PM	
5 PM	
6 PM	
7 PM	
8 PM	
9 PM	
10 PM	
11 PM	
12 AM	

I give today ☆ ☆ ☆ ☆ ☆

Tomorrow morning will be even better because _____

_____

_____

_____

_____

_____

I have to really enjoy the good things because it makes the bad things okay.

EMMA WATSON,
English actor

Date / /

THIS MORNING, I FEEL						AT THE END OF TODAY, I WANT TO FEEL					
	slightly			very			slightly			very	
Calm						Productive					
Rested						Happy					
Cheerful						Fulfilled					
Confident						Inspired					
Focused						Free					
Tired						Relaxed					
Emotional						Strong					
Stressed						In control					
Overwhelmed						Content					
Angry						Relieved					

This morning, I feel _____ because _____

_____

To feel _____ at the end of the day, I will choose to prioritize

1 _____
2 _____
3 _____

Three things I want to accomplish today

1 _____
2 _____
3 _____

To honor my priorities, I will

1 _____
2 _____
3 _____

To complete these goals, I will

1 _____
2 _____
3 _____

THIS IS HOW I PLAN TO USE MY TIME TODAY

5 AM	
6 AM	
7 AM	
8 AM	
9 AM	
10 AM	
11 AM	
12 PM	
1 PM	
2 PM	
3 PM	
4 PM	
5 PM	
6 PM	
7 PM	
8 PM	
9 PM	
10 PM	
11 PM	
12 AM	

I give today ☆ ☆ ☆ ☆ ☆

Tomorrow morning will be even better because _____

_____

_____

_____

_____

_____

_____

Attitude is a little thing that makes a big difference.

WINSTON CHURCHILL,
British prime minister

Date   /   /

THIS MORNING, I FEEL						AT THE END OF TODAY, I WANT TO FEEL					
	slightly			very			slightly			very	
Calm						Productive					
Rested						Happy					
Cheerful						Fulfilled					
Confident						Inspired					
Focused						Free					
Tired						Relaxed					
Emotional						Strong					
Stressed						In control					
Overwhelmed						Content					
Angry						Relieved					

This morning, I feel _____ because _____

_____

To feel _____ at the end of
the day, I will choose to prioritize

1 _____

2 _____

3 _____

Three things I want to accomplish
today

1 _____

2 _____

3 _____

To honor my priorities, I will

1 _____

2 _____

3 _____

To complete these goals, I will

1 _____

2 _____

3 _____

THIS IS HOW I PLAN TO USE MY TIME TODAY

5 AM	
6 AM	
7 AM	
8 AM	
9 AM	
10 AM	
11 AM	
12 PM	
1 PM	
2 PM	
3 PM	
4 PM	
5 PM	
6 PM	
7 PM	
8 PM	
9 PM	
10 PM	
11 PM	
12 AM	

I give today ☆ ☆ ☆ ☆ ☆

Tomorrow morning will be even better because _____

_____

_____

_____

_____

_____

When you arise in the morning, think of what a precious privilege it is to be alive to breathe, to think, to enjoy, to love.

MARCUS AURELIUS,
emperor of Rome

Date / /

THIS MORNING, I FEEL							AT THE END OF TODAY, I WANT TO FEEL						
	slightly				very			slightly				very	
Calm							Productive						
Rested							Happy						
Cheerful							Fulfilled						
Confident							Inspired						
Focused							Free						
Tired							Relaxed						
Emotional							Strong						
Stressed							In control						
Overwhelmed							Content						
Angry							Relieved						

This morning, I feel _____ because _____

_____

To feel _____ at the end of
the day, I will choose to prioritize

1 _____

2 _____

3 _____

To honor my priorities, I will

1 _____

2 _____

3 _____

Three things I want to accomplish
today

1 _____

2 _____

3 _____

To complete these goals, I will

1 _____

2 _____

3 _____

THIS IS HOW I PLAN TO USE MY TIME TODAY

5 AM	
6 AM	
7 AM	
8 AM	
9 AM	
10 AM	
11 AM	
12 PM	
1 PM	
2 PM	
3 PM	
4 PM	
5 PM	
6 PM	
7 PM	
8 PM	
9 PM	
10 PM	
11 PM	
12 AM	

I give today ☆ ☆ ☆ ☆ ☆

Tomorrow morning will be even better because _____

_____

_____

_____

_____

_____

If everything was perfect, you would never learn and you would never grow.

BEYONCÉ KNOWLES,
American singer

Date / /

THIS MORNING, I FEEL	slightly			very		AT THE END OF TODAY, I WANT TO FEEL	slightly			very	
Calm						Productive					
Rested						Happy					
Cheerful						Fulfilled					
Confident						Inspired					
Focused						Free					
Tired						Relaxed					
Emotional						Strong					
Stressed						In control					
Overwhelmed						Content					
Angry						Relieved					

This morning, I feel _____ because _____

_____

To feel _____ at the end of the day, I will choose to prioritize

1 _____

2 _____

3 _____

Three things I want to accomplish today

1 _____

2 _____

3 _____

To honor my priorities, I will

1 _____

2 _____

3 _____

To complete these goals, I will

1 _____

2 _____

3 _____

THIS IS HOW I PLAN TO USE MY TIME TODAY

5 AM	
6 AM	
7 AM	
8 AM	
9 AM	
10 AM	
11 AM	
12 PM	
1 PM	
2 PM	
3 PM	
4 PM	
5 PM	
6 PM	
7 PM	
8 PM	
9 PM	
10 PM	
11 PM	
12 AM	

I give today ☆ ☆ ☆ ☆ ☆

Tomorrow morning will be even better because _____

_____

_____

_____

_____

_____

Be about ten times more magnanimous than you believe yourself capable of. Your life will be a hundred times better for it.

CHERYL STRAYED,
American author

Date / /

THIS MORNING, I FEEL		slightly				very	AT THE END OF TODAY, I WANT TO FEEL		slightly				very
Calm							Productive						
Rested							Happy						
Cheerful							Fulfilled						
Confident							Inspired						
Focused							Free						
Tired							Relaxed						
Emotional							Strong						
Stressed							In control						
Overwhelmed							Content						
Angry							Relieved						

This morning, I feel _____ because _____

_____

To feel _____ at the end of the day, I will choose to prioritize

1 _____

2 _____

3 _____

To honor my priorities, I will

1 _____

2 _____

3 _____

Three things I want to accomplish today

1 _____

2 _____

3 _____

To complete these goals, I will

1 _____

2 _____

3 _____

THIS IS HOW I PLAN TO USE MY TIME TODAY

5 AM	
6 AM	
7 AM	
8 AM	
9 AM	
10 AM	
11 AM	
12 PM	
1 PM	
2 PM	
3 PM	
4 PM	
5 PM	
6 PM	
7 PM	
8 PM	
9 PM	
10 PM	
11 PM	
12 AM	

I give today ☆ ☆ ☆ ☆ ☆

Tomorrow morning will be
even better because _____

_____

_____

_____

_____

_____

*Our greatness
has always come
from people who
expect nothing
and take nothing
for granted.*

MICHELLE OBAMA,
*forty-fourth first lady
of the United States*

Date / /

THIS MORNING, I FEEL	slightly			very			AT THE END OF TODAY, I WANT TO FEEL	slightly			very	
Calm							Productive					
Rested							Happy					
Cheerful							Fulfilled					
Confident							Inspired					
Focused							Free					
Tired							Relaxed					
Emotional							Strong					
Stressed							In control					
Overwhelmed							Content					
Angry							Relieved					

This morning, I feel _____ because _____

_____

To feel _____ at the end of the day, I will choose to prioritize

1 _____

2 _____

3 _____

Three things I want to accomplish today

1 _____

2 _____

3 _____

To honor my priorities, I will

1 _____

2 _____

3 _____

To complete these goals, I will

1 _____

2 _____

3 _____

THIS IS HOW I PLAN TO USE MY TIME TODAY

5 AM	
6 AM	
7 AM	
8 AM	
9 AM	
10 AM	
11 AM	
12 PM	
1 PM	
2 PM	
3 PM	
4 PM	
5 PM	
6 PM	
7 PM	
8 PM	
9 PM	
10 PM	
11 PM	
12 AM	

I give today ☆ ☆ ☆ ☆ ☆

Tomorrow morning will be
even better because _____

_____

_____

_____

_____

_____

*Today's goals:
coffee and
kindness. Maybe
two coffees, and
then kindness.*

NANEA HOFFMAN,
American writer and
blogger

Date / /

THIS MORNING, I FEEL	slightly			very		AT THE END OF TODAY, I WANT TO FEEL	slightly			very	
Calm						Productive					
Rested						Happy					
Cheerful						Fulfilled					
Confident						Inspired					
Focused						Free					
Tired						Relaxed					
Emotional						Strong					
Stressed						In control					
Overwhelmed						Content					
Angry						Relieved					

This morning, I feel _____ because _____

_____

To feel _____ at the end of the day, I will choose to prioritize

1 _____

2 _____

3 _____

To honor my priorities, I will

1 _____

2 _____

3 _____

Three things I want to accomplish today

1 _____

2 _____

3 _____

To complete these goals, I will

1 _____

2 _____

3 _____

THIS IS HOW I PLAN TO USE MY TIME TODAY

5 AM	
6 AM	
7 AM	
8 AM	
9 AM	
10 AM	
11 AM	
12 PM	
1 PM	
2 PM	
3 PM	
4 PM	
5 PM	
6 PM	
7 PM	
8 PM	
9 PM	
10 PM	
11 PM	
12 AM	

I give today ☆ ☆ ☆ ☆ ☆

Tomorrow morning will be
even better because _____

_____

_____

_____

_____

_____

*An early-
morning walk
is a blessing for
the whole day.*

HENRY DAVID THOREAU,
American poet and essayist

Date / /

THIS MORNING, I FEEL						AT THE END OF TODAY, I WANT TO FEEL					
	slightly			very			slightly			very	
Calm						Productive					
Rested						Happy					
Cheerful						Fulfilled					
Confident						Inspired					
Focused						Free					
Tired						Relaxed					
Emotional						Strong					
Stressed						In control					
Overwhelmed						Content					
Angry						Relieved					

This morning, I feel _____ because _____

_____

To feel _____ at the end of the day, I will choose to prioritize

1 _____

2 _____

3 _____

To honor my priorities, I will

1 _____

2 _____

3 _____

Three things I want to accomplish today

1 _____

2 _____

3 _____

To complete these goals, I will

1 _____

2 _____

3 _____

THIS IS HOW I PLAN TO USE MY TIME TODAY

5 AM	
6 AM	
7 AM	
8 AM	
9 AM	
10 AM	
11 AM	
12 PM	
1 PM	
2 PM	
3 PM	
4 PM	
5 PM	
6 PM	
7 PM	
8 PM	
9 PM	
10 PM	
11 PM	
12 AM	

I give today ☆ ☆ ☆ ☆ ☆

Tomorrow morning will be
even better because _____

_____

_____

_____

_____

_____

*Every morning,
I wake up saying,
"I'm still alive, a
miracle." And so I
keep on pushing.*

JIM CARREY,
*Canadian-American
actor and comedian*

Date / /

THIS MORNING, I FEEL	slightly	very	AT THE END OF TODAY, I WANT TO FEEL	slightly	very
Calm			Productive		
Rested			Happy		
Cheerful			Fulfilled		
Confident			Inspired		
Focused			Free		
Tired			Relaxed		
Emotional			Strong		
Stressed			In control		
Overwhelmed			Content		
Angry			Relieved		

This morning, I feel _____ because _____

_____

To feel _____ at the end of the day, I will choose to prioritize

1 _____
2 _____
3 _____

Three things I want to accomplish today

1 _____
2 _____
3 _____

To honor my priorities, I will

1 _____
2 _____
3 _____

To complete these goals, I will

1 _____
2 _____
3 _____

THIS IS HOW I PLAN TO USE MY TIME TODAY

5 AM	
6 AM	
7 AM	
8 AM	
9 AM	
10 AM	
11 AM	
12 PM	
1 PM	
2 PM	
3 PM	
4 PM	
5 PM	
6 PM	
7 PM	
8 PM	
9 PM	
10 PM	
11 PM	
12 AM	

I give today ☆ ☆ ☆ ☆ ☆

Tomorrow morning will be even better because _____

_____

_____

_____

_____

_____

Smile in the mirror. Do that every morning and you'll start to see a big difference in your life.

YOKO ONO,
Japanese artist and activist

Date / /

THIS MORNING, I FEEL		slightly			very		AT THE END OF TODAY, I WANT TO FEEL		slightly			very	
Calm							Productive						
Rested							Happy						
Cheerful							Fulfilled						
Confident							Inspired						
Focused							Free						
Tired							Relaxed						
Emotional							Strong						
Stressed							In control						
Overwhelmed							Content						
Angry							Relieved						

This morning, I feel _____ because _____

_____

To feel _____ at the end of the day, I will choose to prioritize

1 _____

2 _____

3 _____

Three things I want to accomplish today

1 _____

2 _____

3 _____

To honor my priorities, I will

1 _____

2 _____

3 _____

To complete these goals, I will

1 _____

2 _____

3 _____

THIS IS HOW I PLAN TO USE MY TIME TODAY

5 AM	
6 AM	
7 AM	
8 AM	
9 AM	
10 AM	
11 AM	
12 PM	
1 PM	
2 PM	
3 PM	
4 PM	
5 PM	
6 PM	
7 PM	
8 PM	
9 PM	
10 PM	
11 PM	
12 AM	

I give today ☆ ☆ ☆ ☆ ☆

Tomorrow morning will be even better because _____

_____

_____

_____

_____

_____

Some people dream of success, while other people get up every morning and make it happen.

WAYNE HUIZENGA,
American businessman

Date / /

THIS MORNING, I FEEL							AT THE END OF TODAY, I WANT TO FEEL						
	slightly			very				slightly			very		
Calm							Productive						
Rested							Happy						
Cheerful							Fulfilled						
Confident							Inspired						
Focused							Free						
Tired							Relaxed						
Emotional							Strong						
Stressed							In control						
Overwhelmed							Content						
Angry							Relieved						

This morning, I feel _____ because _____

_____

To feel _____ at the end of the day, I will choose to prioritize

1 _____

2 _____

3 _____

To honor my priorities, I will

1 _____

2 _____

3 _____

Three things I want to accomplish today

1 _____

2 _____

3 _____

To complete these goals, I will

1 _____

2 _____

3 _____

THIS IS HOW I PLAN TO USE MY TIME TODAY

5 AM	
6 AM	
7 AM	
8 AM	
9 AM	
10 AM	
11 AM	
12 PM	
1 PM	
2 PM	
3 PM	
4 PM	
5 PM	
6 PM	
7 PM	
8 PM	
9 PM	
10 PM	
11 PM	
12 AM	

I give today ☆ ☆ ☆ ☆ ☆

Tomorrow morning will be even better because _____

_____

_____

_____

_____

_____

Morning comes whether you set the alarm or not.

URSULA K. LE GUIN,
American author

Date / /

THIS MORNING, I FEEL				slightly			very		AT THE END OF TODAY, I WANT TO FEEL				slightly			very
Calm									Productive							
Rested									Happy							
Cheerful									Fulfilled							
Confident									Inspired							
Focused									Free							
Tired									Relaxed							
Emotional									Strong							
Stressed									In control							
Overwhelmed									Content							
Angry									Relieved							

This morning, I feel _____ because _____

_____

To feel _____ at the end of the day, I will choose to prioritize

1 _____

2 _____

3 _____

To honor my priorities, I will

1 _____

2 _____

3 _____

Three things I want to accomplish today

1 _____

2 _____

3 _____

To complete these goals, I will

1 _____

2 _____

3 _____

THIS IS HOW I PLAN TO USE MY TIME TODAY

5 AM	
6 AM	
7 AM	
8 AM	
9 AM	
10 AM	
11 AM	
12 PM	
1 PM	
2 PM	
3 PM	
4 PM	
5 PM	
6 PM	
7 PM	
8 PM	
9 PM	
10 PM	
11 PM	
12 AM	

I give today ☆ ☆ ☆ ☆ ☆

Tomorrow morning will be
even better because _____

_____

_____

_____

_____

_____

*Morning is an
important time of
day, because how you
spend your morning
can often tell you
what kind of day you
are going to have.*

LEMONY SNICKET,
*pen name of American
author Daniel Handler*

Date / /

THIS MORNING, I FEEL						
	slightly					very
Calm						
Rested						
Cheerful						
Confident						
Focused						
Tired						
Emotional						
Stressed						
Overwhelmed						
Angry						

AT THE END OF TODAY, I WANT TO FEEL						
	slightly					very
Productive						
Happy						
Fulfilled						
Inspired						
Free						
Relaxed						
Strong						
In control						
Content						
Relieved						

This morning, I feel _____ because _____

_____

To feel _____ at the end of the day, I will choose to prioritize

1 _____
2 _____
3 _____

Three things I want to accomplish today

1 _____
2 _____
3 _____

To honor my priorities, I will

1 _____
2 _____
3 _____

To complete these goals, I will

1 _____
2 _____
3 _____

THIS IS HOW I PLAN TO USE MY TIME TODAY

5 AM	
6 AM	
7 AM	
8 AM	
9 AM	
10 AM	
11 AM	
12 PM	
1 PM	
2 PM	
3 PM	
4 PM	
5 PM	
6 PM	
7 PM	
8 PM	
9 PM	
10 PM	
11 PM	
12 AM	

I give today ☆ ☆ ☆ ☆ ☆

Tomorrow morning will be even better because _____

_____

_____

_____

_____

I'm always thinking about creating. My future starts when I wake up every morning. Every day I find something creative to do with my life.

MILES DAVIS,
American jazz musician

Date / /

THIS MORNING, I FEEL				AT THE END OF TODAY, I WANT TO FEEL			
	slightly	very			slightly	very	
Calm				Productive			
Rested				Happy			
Cheerful				Fulfilled			
Confident				Inspired			
Focused				Free			
Tired				Relaxed			
Emotional				Strong			
Stressed				In control			
Overwhelmed				Content			
Angry				Relieved			

This morning, I feel _____ because _____

_____

To feel _____ at the end of the day, I will choose to prioritize

1 _____

2 _____

3 _____

Three things I want to accomplish today

1 _____

2 _____

3 _____

To honor my priorities, I will

1 _____

2 _____

3 _____

To complete these goals, I will

1 _____

2 _____

3 _____

THIS IS HOW I PLAN TO USE MY TIME TODAY

5 AM	
6 AM	
7 AM	
8 AM	
9 AM	
10 AM	
11 AM	
12 PM	
1 PM	
2 PM	
3 PM	
4 PM	
5 PM	
6 PM	
7 PM	
8 PM	
9 PM	
10 PM	
11 PM	
12 AM	

I give today ☆ ☆ ☆ ☆ ☆

Tomorrow morning will be even better because _____

_____

_____

_____

_____

_____

Now that your eyes are open, make the sun jealous with your burning passion to start the day. Make the sun jealous or stay in bed.

MALAK EL HALABI,
Lebanese poet

Date / /

THIS MORNING, I FEEL	slightly			very		AT THE END OF TODAY, I WANT TO FEEL	slightly			very	
Calm						Productive					
Rested						Happy					
Cheerful						Fulfilled					
Confident						Inspired					
Focused						Free					
Tired						Relaxed					
Emotional						Strong					
Stressed						In control					
Overwhelmed						Content					
Angry						Relieved					

This morning, I feel _____ because _____
_____

To feel _____ at the end of
the day, I will choose to prioritize

1 _____
2 _____
3 _____

Three things I want to accomplish
today

1 _____
2 _____
3 _____

To honor my priorities, I will

1 _____
2 _____
3 _____

To complete these goals, I will

1 _____
2 _____
3 _____

THIS IS HOW I PLAN TO USE MY TIME TODAY

5 AM	
6 AM	
7 AM	
8 AM	
9 AM	
10 AM	
11 AM	
12 PM	
1 PM	
2 PM	
3 PM	
4 PM	
5 PM	
6 PM	
7 PM	
8 PM	
9 PM	
10 PM	
11 PM	
12 AM	

I give today ☆ ☆ ☆ ☆ ☆

Tomorrow morning will be even better because _____

_____

_____

_____

_____

_____

First thing every morning before you arise say out loud, "I believe," three times.

OVID,
Roman poet

Date / /

THIS MORNING, I FEEL						AT THE END OF TODAY, I WANT TO FEEL					
	slightly			very			slightly			very	
Calm						Productive					
Rested						Happy					
Cheerful						Fulfilled					
Confident						Inspired					
Focused						Free					
Tired						Relaxed					
Emotional						Strong					
Stressed						In control					
Overwhelmed						Content					
Angry						Relieved					

This morning, I feel _____ because _____

_____

To feel _____ at the end of
the day, I will choose to prioritize

1 _____

2 _____

3 _____

To honor my priorities, I will

1 _____

2 _____

3 _____

Three things I want to accomplish
today

1 _____

2 _____

3 _____

To complete these goals, I will

1 _____

2 _____

3 _____

THIS IS HOW I PLAN TO USE MY TIME TODAY

5 AM	
6 AM	
7 AM	
8 AM	
9 AM	
10 AM	
11 AM	
12 PM	
1 PM	
2 PM	
3 PM	
4 PM	
5 PM	
6 PM	
7 PM	
8 PM	
9 PM	
10 PM	
11 PM	
12 AM	

I give today ☆ ☆ ☆ ☆ ☆

Tomorrow morning will be even better because _____

_____

_____

_____

_____

_____

I remind myself every morning: Nothing I say this day will teach me anything. So if I'm going to learn, I must do it by listening.

LARRY KING,
American TV host

Date / /

THIS MORNING, I FEEL	slightly			very	AT THE END OF TODAY, I WANT TO FEEL	slightly			very
Calm					Productive				
Rested					Happy				
Cheerful					Fulfilled				
Confident					Inspired				
Focused					Free				
Tired					Relaxed				
Emotional					Strong				
Stressed					In control				
Overwhelmed					Content				
Angry					Relieved				

This morning, I feel _____ because _____

_____

To feel _____ at the end of
the day, I will choose to prioritize

1 _____

2 _____

3 _____

To honor my priorities, I will

1 _____

2 _____

3 _____

Three things I want to accomplish
today

1 _____

2 _____

3 _____

To complete these goals, I will

1 _____

2 _____

3 _____

THIS IS HOW I PLAN TO USE MY TIME TODAY

5 AM	
6 AM	
7 AM	
8 AM	
9 AM	
10 AM	
11 AM	
12 PM	
1 PM	
2 PM	
3 PM	
4 PM	
5 PM	
6 PM	
7 PM	
8 PM	
9 PM	
10 PM	
11 PM	
12 AM	

I give today ☆ ☆ ☆ ☆ ☆

Tomorrow morning will be even better because _____

_____

_____

_____

_____

_____

If you get up in the morning and think the future is going to be better, it is a bright day. Otherwise, it's not.

ELON MUSK,
American businessman

Date / /

THIS MORNING, I FEEL						AT THE END OF TODAY, I WANT TO FEEL					
	slightly			very				slightly			very
Calm						Productive					
Rested						Happy					
Cheerful						Fulfilled					
Confident						Inspired					
Focused						Free					
Tired						Relaxed					
Emotional						Strong					
Stressed						In control					
Overwhelmed						Content					
Angry						Relieved					

This morning, I feel _____ because _____

_____

To feel _____ at the end of the day, I will choose to prioritize

1 _____

2 _____

3 _____

Three things I want to accomplish today

1 _____

2 _____

3 _____

To honor my priorities, I will

1 _____

2 _____

3 _____

To complete these goals, I will

1 _____

2 _____

3 _____

THIS IS HOW I PLAN TO USE MY TIME TODAY

5 AM	
6 AM	
7 AM	
8 AM	
9 AM	
10 AM	
11 AM	
12 PM	
1 PM	
2 PM	
3 PM	
4 PM	
5 PM	
6 PM	
7 PM	
8 PM	
9 PM	
10 PM	
11 PM	
12 AM	

I give today ☆ ☆ ☆ ☆ ☆

Tomorrow morning will be even better because _____

_____

_____

_____

_____

_____

You know that feeling when you wake up in the morning and you're excited for the day? That's one of my main goals in life.

KIRSTEN DUNST,
American actor

Date / /

THIS MORNING, I FEEL						AT THE END OF TODAY, I WANT TO FEEL					
	slightly			very			slightly			very	
Calm						Productive					
Rested						Happy					
Cheerful						Fulfilled					
Confident						Inspired					
Focused						Free					
Tired						Relaxed					
Emotional						Strong					
Stressed						In control					
Overwhelmed						Content					
Angry						Relieved					

This morning, I feel _____ because _____

_____

To feel _____ at the end of the day, I will choose to prioritize

1 _____

2 _____

3 _____

Three things I want to accomplish today

1 _____

2 _____

3 _____

To honor my priorities, I will

1 _____

2 _____

3 _____

To complete these goals, I will

1 _____

2 _____

3 _____

THIS IS HOW I PLAN TO USE MY TIME TODAY

5 AM	
6 AM	
7 AM	
8 AM	
9 AM	
10 AM	
11 AM	
12 PM	
1 PM	
2 PM	
3 PM	
4 PM	
5 PM	
6 PM	
7 PM	
8 PM	
9 PM	
10 PM	
11 PM	
12 AM	

I give today ☆ ☆ ☆ ☆ ☆

Tomorrow morning will be even better because _____

_____

_____

_____

_____

_____

I learned to love myself, because I sleep with myself every night and I wake up with myself every morning, and if I don't like myself, there's no reason to even live the life.

GABOUREY SIDIBE,
American actor

Date / /

THIS MORNING, I FEEL				AT THE END OF TODAY, I WANT TO FEEL				
	slightly		very			slightly		very
Calm				Productive				
Rested				Happy				
Cheerful				Fulfilled				
Confident				Inspired				
Focused				Free				
Tired				Relaxed				
Emotional				Strong				
Stressed				In control				
Overwhelmed				Content				
Angry				Relieved				

This morning, I feel _____ because _____

_____

To feel _____ at the end of
the day, I will choose to prioritize

1 _____

2 _____

3 _____

Three things I want to accomplish
today

1 _____

2 _____

3 _____

To honor my priorities, I will

1 _____

2 _____

3 _____

To complete these goals, I will

1 _____

2 _____

3 _____

THIS IS HOW I PLAN TO USE MY TIME TODAY

5 AM	
6 AM	
7 AM	
8 AM	
9 AM	
10 AM	
11 AM	
12 PM	
1 PM	
2 PM	
3 PM	
4 PM	
5 PM	
6 PM	
7 PM	
8 PM	
9 PM	
10 PM	
11 PM	
12 AM	

I give today ☆ ☆ ☆ ☆ ☆

Tomorrow morning will be even better because _____

_____

_____

_____

_____

_____

Every morning, my dad would have me looking in the mirror and repeat, "Today is going to be a great day; I can, and I will."

GINA RODRIGUEZ,
American actor

Date / /

THIS MORNING, I FEEL							AT THE END OF TODAY, I WANT TO FEEL						
	slightly			very				slightly			very		
Calm							Productive						
Rested							Happy						
Cheerful							Fulfilled						
Confident							Inspired						
Focused							Free						
Tired							Relaxed						
Emotional							Strong						
Stressed							In control						
Overwhelmed							Content						
Angry							Relieved						

This morning, I feel _____ because _____

_____

To feel _____ at the end of
the day, I will choose to prioritize

1 _____

2 _____

3 _____

Three things I want to accomplish
today

1 _____

2 _____

3 _____

To honor my priorities, I will

1 _____

2 _____

3 _____

To complete these goals, I will

1 _____

2 _____

3 _____

THIS IS HOW I PLAN TO USE MY TIME TODAY

5 AM	
6 AM	
7 AM	
8 AM	
9 AM	
10 AM	
11 AM	
12 PM	
1 PM	
2 PM	
3 PM	
4 PM	
5 PM	
6 PM	
7 PM	
8 PM	
9 PM	
10 PM	
11 PM	
12 AM	

I give today ☆ ☆ ☆ ☆ ☆

Tomorrow morning will be even better because _____

_____

_____

_____

_____

_____

The breeze at dawn has secrets to tell you. Don't go back to sleep.

RUMI,
Persian poet

Date / /

THIS MORNING, I FEEL		slightly			very	AT THE END OF TODAY, I WANT TO FEEL		slightly			very
Calm						Productive					
Rested						Happy					
Cheerful						Fulfilled					
Confident						Inspired					
Focused						Free					
Tired						Relaxed					
Emotional						Strong					
Stressed						In control					
Overwhelmed						Content					
Angry						Relieved					

This morning, I feel _____ because _____

_____

To feel _____ at the end of
the day, I will choose to prioritize

1 _____

2 _____

3 _____

Three things I want to accomplish
today

1 _____

2 _____

3 _____

To honor my priorities, I will

1 _____

2 _____

3 _____

To complete these goals, I will

1 _____

2 _____

3 _____

THIS IS HOW I PLAN TO USE MY TIME TODAY

5 AM	
6 AM	
7 AM	
8 AM	
9 AM	
10 AM	
11 AM	
12 PM	
1 PM	
2 PM	
3 PM	
4 PM	
5 PM	
6 PM	
7 PM	
8 PM	
9 PM	
10 PM	
11 PM	
12 AM	

I give today ☆ ☆ ☆ ☆ ☆

Tomorrow morning will be
even better because _____

_____

_____

_____

_____

_____

*I have always
been delighted at
the prospect of a new
day, a fresh try, one
more start, with perhaps
a bit of magic waiting
somewhere behind
the morning.*

J.B. PRIESTLEY,
English author

Date / /

THIS MORNING, I FEEL		slightly		very	AT THE END OF TODAY, I WANT TO FEEL		slightly		very
Calm					Productive				
Rested					Happy				
Cheerful					Fulfilled				
Confident					Inspired				
Focused					Free				
Tired					Relaxed				
Emotional					Strong				
Stressed					In control				
Overwhelmed					Content				
Angry					Relieved				

This morning, I feel _____ because _____

_____

To feel _____ at the end of the day, I will choose to prioritize

1 _____

2 _____

3 _____

Three things I want to accomplish today

1 _____

2 _____

3 _____

To honor my priorities, I will

1 _____

2 _____

3 _____

To complete these goals, I will

1 _____

2 _____

3 _____

THIS IS HOW I PLAN TO USE MY TIME TODAY

5 AM	
6 AM	
7 AM	
8 AM	
9 AM	
10 AM	
11 AM	
12 PM	
1 PM	
2 PM	
3 PM	
4 PM	
5 PM	
6 PM	
7 PM	
8 PM	
9 PM	
10 PM	
11 PM	
12 AM	

I give today ☆ ☆ ☆ ☆ ☆

Tomorrow morning will be
even better because _____

_____

_____

_____

_____

_____

*When you do
something beautiful
and nobody noticed,
do not be sad. For the
sun every morning is
a beautiful spectacle,
and yet most of the
audience still sleeps.*

JOHN LENNON,
*English singer and
songwriter*

Date / /

THIS MORNING, I FEEL	slightly			very		AT THE END OF TODAY, I WANT TO FEEL	slightly			very	
Calm						Productive					
Rested						Happy					
Cheerful						Fulfilled					
Confident						Inspired					
Focused						Free					
Tired						Relaxed					
Emotional						Strong					
Stressed						In control					
Overwhelmed						Content					
Angry						Relieved					

This morning, I feel _____ because _____

_____

To feel _____ at the end of the day, I will choose to prioritize

1 _____

2 _____

3 _____

To honor my priorities, I will

1 _____

2 _____

3 _____

Three things I want to accomplish today

1 _____

2 _____

3 _____

To complete these goals, I will

1 _____

2 _____

3 _____

THIS IS HOW I PLAN TO USE MY TIME TODAY

5 AM	
6 AM	
7 AM	
8 AM	
9 AM	
10 AM	
11 AM	
12 PM	
1 PM	
2 PM	
3 PM	
4 PM	
5 PM	
6 PM	
7 PM	
8 PM	
9 PM	
10 PM	
11 PM	
12 AM	

I give today ☆ ☆ ☆ ☆ ☆

Tomorrow morning will be even better because _____

_____

_____

_____

_____

_____

I never wake up in the morning and wonder why I am here. I wake up and wonder why I am not making here better.

JEFFREY FRY,
Puerto Rican poet

Date / /

THIS MORNING, I FEEL	slightly			very	AT THE END OF TODAY, I WANT TO FEEL	slightly			very
Calm					Productive				
Rested					Happy				
Cheerful					Fulfilled				
Confident					Inspired				
Focused					Free				
Tired					Relaxed				
Emotional					Strong				
Stressed					In control				
Overwhelmed					Content				
Angry					Relieved				

This morning, I feel _____ because _____

_____

To feel _____ at the end of the day, I will choose to prioritize

1 _____

2 _____

3 _____

To honor my priorities, I will

1 _____

2 _____

3 _____

Three things I want to accomplish today

1 _____

2 _____

3 _____

To complete these goals, I will

1 _____

2 _____

3 _____

THIS IS HOW I PLAN TO USE MY TIME TODAY

5 AM	
6 AM	
7 AM	
8 AM	
9 AM	
10 AM	
11 AM	
12 PM	
1 PM	
2 PM	
3 PM	
4 PM	
5 PM	
6 PM	
7 PM	
8 PM	
9 PM	
10 PM	
11 PM	
12 AM	

I give today ☆ ☆ ☆ ☆ ☆

Tomorrow morning will be even better because _____

_____

_____

_____

_____

_____

When everything seems to be going against you, remember that the airplane takes off against the wind, not with it.

HENRY FORD,
American businessman

Date / /

THIS MORNING, I FEEL						AT THE END OF TODAY, I WANT TO FEEL					
	slightly			very			slightly			very	
Calm						Productive					
Rested						Happy					
Cheerful						Fulfilled					
Confident						Inspired					
Focused						Free					
Tired						Relaxed					
Emotional						Strong					
Stressed						In control					
Overwhelmed						Content					
Angry						Relieved					

This morning, I feel _____ because _____

_____

To feel _____ at the end of the day, I will choose to prioritize

1 _____

2 _____

3 _____

To honor my priorities, I will

1 _____

2 _____

3 _____

Three things I want to accomplish today

1 _____

2 _____

3 _____

To complete these goals, I will

1 _____

2 _____

3 _____

THIS IS HOW I PLAN TO USE MY TIME TODAY

5 AM

6 AM

7 AM

8 AM

9 AM

10 AM

11 AM

12 PM

1 PM

2 PM

3 PM

4 PM

5 PM

6 PM

7 PM

8 PM

9 PM

10 PM

11 PM

12 AM

I give today ☆ ☆ ☆ ☆ ☆

Tomorrow morning will be even better because _____

_____

_____

_____

_____

_____

You may be disappointed if you fail, but you are doomed if you don't try.

BEVERLY SILLS,
American opera singer

Date / /

THIS MORNING, I FEEL						AT THE END OF TODAY, I WANT TO FEEL						
	slightly			very				slightly			very	
Calm						Productive						
Rested						Happy						
Cheerful						Fulfilled						
Confident						Inspired						
Focused						Free						
Tired						Relaxed						
Emotional						Strong						
Stressed						In control						
Overwhelmed						Content						
Angry						Relieved						

This morning, I feel _____ because _____
_____

To feel _____ at the end of
the day, I will choose to prioritize

1 _____
2 _____
3 _____

Three things I want to accomplish
today

1 _____
2 _____
3 _____

To honor my priorities, I will

1 _____
2 _____
3 _____

To complete these goals, I will

1 _____
2 _____
3 _____

THIS IS HOW I PLAN TO USE MY TIME TODAY

5 AM	
6 AM	
7 AM	
8 AM	
9 AM	
10 AM	
11 AM	
12 PM	
1 PM	
2 PM	
3 PM	
4 PM	
5 PM	
6 PM	
7 PM	
8 PM	
9 PM	
10 PM	
11 PM	
12 AM	

I give today ☆ ☆ ☆ ☆ ☆

Tomorrow morning will be even better because _____

_____

_____

_____

_____

_____

For the past 33 years, I have looked in the mirror every morning and asked myself: "If today were the last day of my life, would I want to do what I am about to do today?" And whenever the answer has been "No" for too many days in a row, I know I need to change something.

STEVE JOBS,
American businessman

Date / /

THIS MORNING, I FEEL					AT THE END OF TODAY, I WANT TO FEEL				
	slightly			very		slightly			very
Calm					Productive				
Rested					Happy				
Cheerful					Fulfilled				
Confident					Inspired				
Focused					Free				
Tired					Relaxed				
Emotional					Strong				
Stressed					In control				
Overwhelmed					Content				
Angry					Relieved				

This morning, I feel _____ because _____

_____

To feel _____ at the end of
the day, I will choose to prioritize

1 _____

2 _____

3 _____

To honor my priorities, I will

1 _____

2 _____

3 _____

Three things I want to accomplish
today

1 _____

2 _____

3 _____

To complete these goals, I will

1 _____

2 _____

3 _____

THIS IS HOW I PLAN TO USE MY TIME TODAY

5 AM	
6 AM	
7 AM	
8 AM	
9 AM	
10 AM	
11 AM	
12 PM	
1 PM	
2 PM	
3 PM	
4 PM	
5 PM	
6 PM	
7 PM	
8 PM	
9 PM	
10 PM	
11 PM	
12 AM	

I give today ☆ ☆ ☆ ☆ ☆

Tomorrow morning will be even better because _____

_____

_____

_____

_____

The greatest glory in living lies not in never falling, but in rising every time we fall.

NELSON MANDELA,
first black president of
South Africa and activist

Date / /

THIS MORNING, I FEEL				AT THE END OF TODAY, I WANT TO FEEL				
	slightly		very			slightly		very
Calm				Productive				
Rested				Happy				
Cheerful				Fulfilled				
Confident				Inspired				
Focused				Free				
Tired				Relaxed				
Emotional				Strong				
Stressed				In control				
Overwhelmed				Content				
Angry				Relieved				

This morning, I feel _____ because _____

_____

To feel _____ at the end of the day, I will choose to prioritize

1 _____

2 _____

3 _____

To honor my priorities, I will

1 _____

2 _____

3 _____

Three things I want to accomplish today

1 _____

2 _____

3 _____

To complete these goals, I will

1 _____

2 _____

3 _____

THIS IS HOW I PLAN TO USE MY TIME TODAY

5 AM	
6 AM	
7 AM	
8 AM	
9 AM	
10 AM	
11 AM	
12 PM	
1 PM	
2 PM	
3 PM	
4 PM	
5 PM	
6 PM	
7 PM	
8 PM	
9 PM	
10 PM	
11 PM	
12 AM	

I give today ☆ ☆ ☆ ☆ ☆

Tomorrow morning will be
even better because _____

_____

_____

_____

_____

_____

*The way to get
started is to quit
talking and
begin doing.*

*WALT DISNEY,
American entrepreneur
and animator*

Date / /

THIS MORNING, I FEEL		slightly			very		AT THE END OF TODAY, I WANT TO FEEL		slightly			very	
Calm							Productive						
Rested							Happy						
Cheerful							Fulfilled						
Confident							Inspired						
Focused							Free						
Tired							Relaxed						
Emotional							Strong						
Stressed							In control						
Overwhelmed							Content						
Angry							Relieved						

This morning, I feel _____ because _____

_____

To feel _____ at the end of the day, I will choose to prioritize

1 _____

2 _____

3 _____

To honor my priorities, I will

1 _____

2 _____

3 _____

Three things I want to accomplish today

1 _____

2 _____

3 _____

To complete these goals, I will

1 _____

2 _____

3 _____

THIS IS HOW I PLAN TO USE MY TIME TODAY

5 AM	
6 AM	
7 AM	
8 AM	
9 AM	
10 AM	
11 AM	
12 PM	
1 PM	
2 PM	
3 PM	
4 PM	
5 PM	
6 PM	
7 PM	
8 PM	
9 PM	
10 PM	
11 PM	
12 AM	

I give today ☆ ☆ ☆ ☆ ☆

Tomorrow morning will be even better because _____

_____

_____

_____

_____

_____

_____

If you set your goals ridiculously high and it's a failure, you will fail above everyone else's success.

JAMES CAMERON,
Canadian film director

Date   /   /

THIS MORNING, I FEEL				
	slightly			very
Calm				
Rested				
Cheerful				
Confident				
Focused				
Tired				
Emotional				
Stressed				
Overwhelmed				
Angry				

AT THE END OF TODAY, I WANT TO FEEL				
	slightly			very
Productive				
Happy				
Fulfilled				
Inspired				
Free				
Relaxed				
Strong				
In control				
Content				
Relieved				

This morning, I feel _____ because _____

_____

To feel _____ at the end of
the day, I will choose to prioritize

1 _____

2 _____

3 _____

To honor my priorities, I will

1 _____

2 _____

3 _____

Three things I want to accomplish
today

1 _____

2 _____

3 _____

To complete these goals, I will

1 _____

2 _____

3 _____

THIS IS HOW I PLAN TO USE MY TIME TODAY

5 AM	
6 AM	
7 AM	
8 AM	
9 AM	
10 AM	
11 AM	
12 PM	
1 PM	
2 PM	
3 PM	
4 PM	
5 PM	
6 PM	
7 PM	
8 PM	
9 PM	
10 PM	
11 PM	
12 AM	

I give today ☆ ☆ ☆ ☆ ☆

Tomorrow morning will be even better because _____

_____

_____

_____

_____

_____

Don't judge each day by the harvest you reap but by the seeds that you plant.

ROBERT LOUIS STEVENSON,
Scottish author and poet

Date / /

THIS MORNING, I FEEL	slightly				very		AT THE END OF TODAY, I WANT TO FEEL	slightly				very	
Calm							Productive						
Rested							Happy						
Cheerful							Fulfilled						
Confident							Inspired						
Focused							Free						
Tired							Relaxed						
Emotional							Strong						
Stressed							In control						
Overwhelmed							Content						
Angry							Relieved						

This morning, I feel _____ because _____
_____

To feel _____ at the end of
the day, I will choose to prioritize

1 _____

2 _____

3 _____

Three things I want to accomplish
today

1 _____

2 _____

3 _____

To honor my priorities, I will

1 _____

2 _____

3 _____

To complete these goals, I will

1 _____

2 _____

3 _____

THIS IS HOW I PLAN TO USE MY TIME TODAY

5 AM	
6 AM	
7 AM	
8 AM	
9 AM	
10 AM	
11 AM	
12 PM	
1 PM	
2 PM	
3 PM	
4 PM	
5 PM	
6 PM	
7 PM	
8 PM	
9 PM	
10 PM	
11 PM	
12 AM	

I give today ☆ ☆ ☆ ☆ ☆

Tomorrow morning will be even better because _____

_____

_____

_____

_____

_____

Never let the fear of striking out keep you from playing the game.

BABE RUTH,
American baseball player

Date / /

THIS MORNING, I FEEL	slightly	very	AT THE END OF TODAY, I WANT TO FEEL	slightly	very
Calm			Productive		
Rested			Happy		
Cheerful			Fulfilled		
Confident			Inspired		
Focused			Free		
Tired			Relaxed		
Emotional			Strong		
Stressed			In control		
Overwhelmed			Content		
Angry			Relieved		

This morning, I feel _____ because _____

_____

To feel _____ at the end of the day, I will choose to prioritize

1 _____

2 _____

3 _____

To honor my priorities, I will

1 _____

2 _____

3 _____

Three things I want to accomplish today

1 _____

2 _____

3 _____

To complete these goals, I will

1 _____

2 _____

3 _____

THIS IS HOW I PLAN TO USE MY TIME TODAY

5 AM	
6 AM	
7 AM	
8 AM	
9 AM	
10 AM	
11 AM	
12 PM	
1 PM	
2 PM	
3 PM	
4 PM	
5 PM	
6 PM	
7 PM	
8 PM	
9 PM	
10 PM	
11 PM	
12 AM	

I give today ☆ ☆ ☆ ☆ ☆

Tomorrow morning will be even better because _____

_____

_____

_____

_____

A day without laughter is a day wasted.

CHARLIE CHAPLIN,
English actor and filmmaker

Date / /

THIS MORNING, I FEEL	slightly			very		AT THE END OF TODAY, I WANT TO FEEL	slightly			very	
Calm						Productive					
Rested						Happy					
Cheerful						Fulfilled					
Confident						Inspired					
Focused						Free					
Tired						Relaxed					
Emotional						Strong					
Stressed						In control					
Overwhelmed						Content					
Angry						Relieved					

This morning, I feel _____ because _____

_____

To feel _____ at the end of the day, I will choose to prioritize

1 _____

2 _____

3 _____

Three things I want to accomplish today

1 _____

2 _____

3 _____

To honor my priorities, I will

1 _____

2 _____

3 _____

To complete these goals, I will

1 _____

2 _____

3 _____

THIS IS HOW I PLAN TO USE MY TIME TODAY

5 AM	
6 AM	
7 AM	
8 AM	
9 AM	
10 AM	
11 AM	
12 PM	
1 PM	
2 PM	
3 PM	
4 PM	
5 PM	
6 PM	
7 PM	
8 PM	
9 PM	
10 PM	
11 PM	
12 AM	

I give today ☆ ☆ ☆ ☆ ☆

Tomorrow morning will be
even better because _____

_____

_____

_____

_____

_____

*It is never
too late to be
what you might
have been.*

GEORGE ELIOT,
*pen name of English
author Mary Ann Evans*

Date / /

THIS MORNING, I FEEL		slightly			very		AT THE END OF TODAY, I WANT TO FEEL		slightly			very	
Calm							Productive						
Rested							Happy						
Cheerful							Fulfilled						
Confident							Inspired						
Focused							Free						
Tired							Relaxed						
Emotional							Strong						
Stressed							In control						
Overwhelmed							Content						
Angry							Relieved						

This morning, I feel _____ because _____

_____

To feel _____ at the end of the day, I will choose to prioritize

1 _____

2 _____

3 _____

To honor my priorities, I will

1 _____

2 _____

3 _____

Three things I want to accomplish today

1 _____

2 _____

3 _____

To complete these goals, I will

1 _____

2 _____

3 _____

THIS IS HOW I PLAN TO USE MY TIME TODAY

5 AM	
6 AM	
7 AM	
8 AM	
9 AM	
10 AM	
11 AM	
12 PM	
1 PM	
2 PM	
3 PM	
4 PM	
5 PM	
6 PM	
7 PM	
8 PM	
9 PM	
10 PM	
11 PM	
12 AM	

I give today ☆ ☆ ☆ ☆ ☆

Tomorrow morning will be even better because _____

_____

_____

_____

_____

_____

You can only come to the morning through the shadows.

J.R.R. TOLKIEN,
English philologist
and author

Date / /

THIS MORNING, I FEEL						AT THE END OF TODAY, I WANT TO FEEL					
	slightly			very			slightly			very	
Calm						Productive					
Rested						Happy					
Cheerful						Fulfilled					
Confident						Inspired					
Focused						Free					
Tired						Relaxed					
Emotional						Strong					
Stressed						In control					
Overwhelmed						Content					
Angry						Relieved					

This morning, I feel _____ because _____

_____

To feel _____ at the end of
the day, I will choose to prioritize

1 _____

2 _____

3 _____

To honor my priorities, I will

1 _____

2 _____

3 _____

Three things I want to accomplish
today

1 _____

2 _____

3 _____

To complete these goals, I will

1 _____

2 _____

3 _____

THIS IS HOW I PLAN TO USE MY TIME TODAY

5 AM	
6 AM	
7 AM	
8 AM	
9 AM	
10 AM	
11 AM	
12 PM	
1 PM	
2 PM	
3 PM	
4 PM	
5 PM	
6 PM	
7 PM	
8 PM	
9 PM	
10 PM	
11 PM	
12 AM	

I give today ☆ ☆ ☆ ☆ ☆

Tomorrow morning will be even better because _____

_____

_____

_____

_____

Given another shot at life, I would seize every minute of it...look at it and really see it... try it on...live it...exhaust it...and never give that minute back until there was nothing left of it.

ERMA BOMBECK,
American humorist

Date / /

THIS MORNING, I FEEL					AT THE END OF TODAY, I WANT TO FEEL				
	slightly		very			slightly		very	
Calm					Productive				
Rested					Happy				
Cheerful					Fulfilled				
Confident					Inspired				
Focused					Free				
Tired					Relaxed				
Emotional					Strong				
Stressed					In control				
Overwhelmed					Content				
Angry					Relieved				

This morning, I feel _____ because _____

_____

To feel _____ at the end of the day, I will choose to prioritize

1 _____

2 _____

3 _____

To honor my priorities, I will

1 _____

2 _____

3 _____

Three things I want to accomplish today

1 _____

2 _____

3 _____

To complete these goals, I will

1 _____

2 _____

3 _____

THIS IS HOW I PLAN TO USE MY TIME TODAY

5 AM	
6 AM	
7 AM	
8 AM	
9 AM	
10 AM	
11 AM	
12 PM	
1 PM	
2 PM	
3 PM	
4 PM	
5 PM	
6 PM	
7 PM	
8 PM	
9 PM	
10 PM	
11 PM	
12 AM	

I give today ☆ ☆ ☆ ☆ ☆

Tomorrow morning will be
even better because _____

_____

_____

_____

_____

If you want to make your dreams come true, the first thing you have to do is wake up.

J.M. POWER,
American author

Date / /

THIS MORNING, I FEEL	slightly			very	AT THE END OF TODAY, I WANT TO FEEL	slightly			very
Calm					Productive				
Rested					Happy				
Cheerful					Fulfilled				
Confident					Inspired				
Focused					Free				
Tired					Relaxed				
Emotional					Strong				
Stressed					In control				
Overwhelmed					Content				
Angry					Relieved				

This morning, I feel _____ because _____

_____

To feel _____ at the end of the day, I will choose to prioritize

1 _____

2 _____

3 _____

To honor my priorities, I will

1 _____

2 _____

3 _____

Three things I want to accomplish today

1 _____

2 _____

3 _____

To complete these goals, I will

1 _____

2 _____

3 _____

THIS IS HOW I PLAN TO USE MY TIME TODAY

5 AM	
6 AM	
7 AM	
8 AM	
9 AM	
10 AM	
11 AM	
12 PM	
1 PM	
2 PM	
3 PM	
4 PM	
5 PM	
6 PM	
7 PM	
8 PM	
9 PM	
10 PM	
11 PM	
12 AM	

I give today ☆ ☆ ☆ ☆ ☆

Tomorrow morning will be
even better because _____

_____

_____

_____

_____

_____

Your attitude is like a box of crayons that color your world. Constantly color your picture gray, and your picture will always be bleak. Try adding some bright colors to the picture by including humor, and your picture begins to lighten up.

ALLEN KLEIN,
American businessman